# Apologetics

Michael Sheehan

Albatross Publishers
Naples, Italy
2020

*Originally Published in Dublin by M. H. Gill & Son, 1925*

ISBN 978-1-946963-47-5

# APOLOGETICS

BY

The Most Rev. M. SHEEHAN, D.D.
COADJUTOR ARCHBISHOP OF SYDNEY.
*Formerly of St. Patrick's College, Maynooth.*

DUBLIN
M. H. GILL & SON, LTD., 50 UPPER O'CONNELL STREET
1925

*Dublini, die 15° Novembris, 1918.*

# CONTENTS.

|  | PAGE |
|---|---|
| INTRODUCTION | vi |
| CHAPTER I.—THE EXISTENCE OF GOD | 1 |
| CHAPTER II.—THE HUMAN SOUL: ITS SPIRITUALITY AND IMMORTALITY | 25 |
| CHAPTER III.—NATURAL RELIGION: ITS INSUFFICIENCY. PROBABILITY OF REVELATION | 31 |
| CHAPTER IV.—THE SIGNS OF REVELATION: MIRACLES AND PROPHECY | 35 |
| CHAPTER V.—THE HISTORICAL VALUE OF THE GOSPELS, THE ACTS OF THE APOSTLES, AND THE EPISTLES OF ST. PAUL | 40 |
| CHAPTER VI.—JESUS CHRIST CLAIMED TO BE GOD | 49 |
| CHAPTER VII.—JESUS CHRIST, TRUE GOD | 54 |
| CHAPTER VIII.—JESUS CHRIST FOUNDED A CHURCH | 74 |
| CHAPTER IX.—THE CHARACTERISTICS OF THE CHURCH OF CHRIST | 79 |
| CHAPTER X.—THE IDENTIFICATION OF THE CHURCH OF CHRIST | 94 |
| CHAPTER XI.—THE GOVERNMENT OF THE CHURCH OF CHRIST | 118 |
| SUPPLEMENTARY NOTES | 138 |
| INDEX | 139 |

## SEQUENCE OF THE ARGUMENT

1. God exists; He is the Supreme Being, intelligent and free, infinite in all perfections; He created the world and all things in it (Ch. I.).—2. Man, one of God's creatures, possesses reason and free-will (Ch. II.). Man has duties to God, to himself, and to his neighbour; without a revelation, it would be practically impossible for the generality of mankind to arrive at a full knowledge of these duties, and of the truths that underlie them; we have, therefore, an assurance that God in His mercy must, as a fact, have given the necessary revelation (Ch. III.); miracles and prophecies are signs by which a divine revelation can be known with certainty (Ch. IV.).—3. We examine the claims of Christianity to be a divine revelation. We find that its sacred books are, as history, trustworthy (Ch. V.), and that they prove the following: (a) they prove that Christ claimed to be God (Ch. VI.), and made good His claim by miracles and prophecies (Ch. VII.); (b) they prove that He established a Church, and invested her, and her alone, with authority to teach His doctrine to mankind (Ch. VIII.)—it follows, therefore, that all rival institutions and all rival doctrines must be false (p. 115); (c) they prove that the Church founded by Christ had certain characteristics, one of which was imperishability: His Church, therefore, still exists in the world (Ch. IX.).—4. Of the existing Christian Churches, the Catholic Church is the only one that possesses the characteristics of the institution founded by Christ. Therefore, the Catholic Church is the one and only true Church (Ch. X.)—*N.B.* Ch. XI. on the Primacy and Infallibility of the Pope does not belong to Apologetics. It has been inserted to complete the treatise on the Church.

# INTRODUCTION.

*Summary.*

    Apologetics defined; its relation to Catholic Doctrine; its study, a duty and a discipline.

    The nature of the proof we employ in Apologetics: conclusive, but not coercive.

    First Principles.

**Apologetics.** DEFINITION. RELATION TO CATHOLIC DOCTRINE.—Apologetics is the science concerned with the defence of the Christian religion. It proves the existence of God, the spirituality of the human soul, the Divinity of Christ, and the authority of the Church which He founded. It takes us through a series of connected truths, and concludes that the one and only guide of faith on earth is the Catholic Church, Holy and Infallible. It leads us to the portals of the House of God, and bids us enter. Within, we hear the Catholic Doctrine, Christ's message to us as interpreted by His living representative.

ITS STUDY, A DUTY AND A DISCIPLINE.—We who, in common with the least learned of our communion, see in the marvellous growth of the Church, in her solid unity, in her unconquerable stability, in her wondrous holiness, and in her inexhaustible fruitfulness in all charitable works, an abiding and conclusive testimony to her Divine mission, cannot read this treatise on Apologetics in a spirit of doubt or hostility. We do not question her claims; we do not wish, and we do not need, to find or strengthen conviction, by any elaborate course of argument; possessed of the grace-given certainty of faith, we will never waver in our love and veneration for her as the Mother of all blessings. But we live in an age hostile to God, to Christ, and to His Church, and we must be prepared, when challenged, to prove that our faith rests on a basis which must commend itself as reasonable to any unprejudiced mind. The exhortation of St. Peter to the early Christians to be "ready always to satisfy every one that asketh you a reason of that hope which is in you," (1 Peter iii. 15), is as applicable to us as it was to them. The study of Apologetics brings with it the twofold reward of a duty fulfilled and of a valuable mental discipline acquired. It stimulates and develops our reasoning powers by setting them to work at problems of profound importance and unfailing interest.

**Our Proof.** ITS NATURE.—The youthful reader, too much impressed, perhaps, by the methods he has seen employed in mathematics and physical science, must be warned against the assumption that, outside the sphere of exact calculation and experiment, absolute certainty is unattainable. On reflection, he will realize that, by inference from facts, he can build up a solid edifice of truth. For instance, he can form an accurate estimate of a lawgiver's wisdom from the effects of his legislation; and he can prove the genius of a Michael Angelo, or a Napoleon, by studying the artistic creations of the one, or the strategy of the other. From effects he can argue with certainty to their cause, even though the cause be a something to which no mathematical or experimental test can be applied.

CONCLUSIVE BUT NOT COERCIVE.—Our proof is conclusive. That is, it is sufficient to exclude all reasonable doubt. But it is not coercive. It cannot force conviction on the prejudiced or the foolish, for prejudice and folly are forces against which it is futile to contend. Thus, it is waste of time to argue with one who refuses to listen, or with one who seriously defends an absurdity, who maintains, *e.g.*, that a great work of literature is a mere chance arrangement of words, or that thieving and drunkenness are not vices. Folly is mere imbecility, mere incapacity of understanding, while prejudice acts like a brake on the reason, impeding its natural movement. Manifestly, then, a perfectly valid proof may not carry conviction to all. It deserves, but does not receive, universal assent.

**First Principles.**—First Principles are the self-evident truths that serve as the basis of a science. Thus, in Euclid, the axioms are the First Principles from which all the propositions may ultimately be deduced. In our treatise, the First Principles are chiefly two, viz., (1) that our reason and the evidence of our senses are trustworthy, and (2) that anything which begins to exist must have been brought into existence by something distinct from itself (Principle of Causality). We need not, and, in fact, we cannot prove First Principles. They shine by their own light. Those who deny their validity put themselves beyond the pale of discussion.

# CHAPTER I.

## THE EXISTENCE OF GOD.

*We prove by the following arguments the existence of a Living, Personal God, i.e. of a Being endowed with intelligence and free-will, the First or Ultimate Cause of all things distinct from Himself.*

### I. ARGUMENT FROM THE LAWS OF NATURE.

#### § 1.—*Brief treatment.*

All nature is obedient to law. Astronomy, physics, and chemistry show that inanimate matter, from the stars of heaven to the smallest speck of dust, is, in all its movements and changes, subject to fixed laws. The same holds for living things—plants, animals, and men: each species grows, develops, and acts in the same way. The entire universe is bound together into one vastly complicated whole, and is like a great machine the parts of which are admirably fitted together. The orderly movement of the heavens, the marvellous structure of living things and their organs, such as the organs of sight and hearing, the wonderful instinct of the lower animals, as instanced in the work of bees and the nest-building of birds, the great achievements of man in science, literature, and art—all these marvels are the outcome of the laws of nature.

It is unthinkable that laws, producing effects so vast, and yet so orderly in their entirety and in their smallest detail, could have sprung from chance, or from any unintelligent cause we choose to name. They must have been imposed by a wise Lawgiver who so framed them, and so directed them in their working as to achieve the ends he desired. That Lawgiver must be a being of vast intelligence  He must possess free-will, for he has given that faculty to man. He must himself be God, or depend ultimately on one who is God, the First Cause of all things.

*Objections.*

(1) The advocates of Materialist Evolution assert that the world with all its marvels is due ultimately to the working of physical and chemical laws, to a mere motion of matter.—Reply: (*a*) The theory does not account for the origin of motion, life, sensation, reason. (*b*) It proposes the gross absurdity that mere lifeless forces, under no intelligent direction, could have produced, in man, works of the highest intelligence.

(2) "The existence of evil in the world, and the prodigality of nature seem to argue against the wisdom of the Lawgiver." Reply: The notion that there are defects in the work of the Lawgiver is due, not to the imperfect character of His design, but to our imperfect understanding of it.

## § 2.—*Fuller treatment.*

**All Nature is obedient to law.**[1]—That the universe is obedient to law is a truth which forms the very basis of all physical science:—

(1) Inanimate matter is subject to law:—(*a*) In Astronomy, the laws of Kepler and Newton have exhibited the heavens as forming so exact a mechanical system that seemingly irregular occurrences, such as eclipses and the return of comets, can be predicted with certainty. (*b*) In Physics, the laws of sound, heat, light, and electricity, work so perfectly that results can be calculated in advance with mathematical accuracy. (*c*) In Chemistry, atoms are found to have definite attractions and affinities and to combine

---

[1] A law of nature, or physical law, may be merely a formal statement of what regularly occurs in nature, or it may denote the cause of such regularity. We use the expression in the latter sense. It must not be inferred, however, that we claim any exact knowledge of the cause of each set of regularly occurring phenomena. That the cause exists, we are certain, but as to its precise nature and mode of operation we need not profess to know anything.

according to fixed laws. In all other branches and sub-divisions of physical science, the same regularity is observed. Everywhere, like agents in like circumstances produce the same effects.

(2) Animate matter is subject to law:—(a) All living things are subject to fixed laws of nutrition, growth, and reproduction. Plants, animals, and men develop from a single living cell. In the higher forms of life, in man, for instance, that cell multiplies itself many times, gradually building up a great complexity of organs, such as the eye, the ear, the heart and lungs. (b) Every living thing possesses the capacity to repair its worn parts. (c) Among the lower animals, every individual of the same species is endowed with the same set of useful appetites and tendencies in connection with the quest for food, the defence of life, the propagation of its kind, and the care of its offspring. (d) The same holds for man, who, in addition, possesses inclinations in keeping with his rational nature. Impelled by the desire for truth and the love of beauty, his mind builds up many wonderful sciences, and produces all the marvels of literature and art. In its movements it is subject to certain laws, the laws of thought, just as the seed, developing into stem, leaf, and flower, is subject to the laws of growth.

(3) Animate matter is subject to, and served by, the laws of inanimate matter:—(a) All living things are subject to the laws of inanimate matter. Nutrition, growth, and many other processes take place in accordance with the laws of chemistry. The laws of gravitation and energy are as valid for the living as for the non-living. The tree, for instance, which stores up the energy of the sun's rays, returns it later on when its withered branches burn on the hearth.

(b) Animate matter is served by the laws of inanimate matter. Examples:—Gravitation has so placed the earth in relation to the sun that it receives the moderate quantity of light and heat necessary for the support of organic life. . . . The air contains in every 100 parts nearly 79 of nitrogen and 21 of oxygen gas, together with ·04 of carbonic acid, a minute proportion of ammonia and other constituents, and a variable quantity of watery vapour. In pure nitrogen, man would suffocate; in pure oxygen, his body would burn out rapidly like a piece of tinder; without carbonic acid, plant-life would be impossible. . . . The plant exhales oxygen and inhales carbonic acid; the animal exhales carbonic acid, and inhales oxygen: thus, each ministers to the life of the other. . . . The water, drawn by evaporation from the sea, drifts in clouds, and descends in rain on the mountains, thus feeding the wells, the streams and rivers, so necessary for living things. . . . Bodies contract with a fall of temperature, and yet water expands when its temperature falls below 4° Centigrade. Hence, ice is lighter than water, and forms a surface-covering which, being of low conductivity, prevents the rapid congealing of the entire body of water and the destruction of living things beneath.

(4) The whole universe, we may say in conclusion, is guided by law. Everywhere there is order.[2] Everywhere there is admirable arrangement. Everywhere there are fixed modes of action.

**The laws of nature could not have been produced by chance or by a cause acting blindly, which is but another name for chance.**—Is it necessary to refute the absurdity that chance could have generated a law? Law is the exact opposite of chance. Fixity is the characteristic of law; variability, the characteristic of chance: (1) Four rods of equal length, flung aimlessly from the hand, may fall into the exact form of a square. It is barely conceivable that this may happen once or twice; it is utterly inconceivable that it should happen a hundred times in unbroken succession; but what should be thought of the conceivability of of its *never* happening otherwise?[3] Yet this last must be realized in order to give us the basis of a law. (2) If the generation by chance of such a simple law be impossible, how can we measure the absurdity of supposing that chance could have produced the vast complexity of laws that rule the universe, the laws whose operation guides the course of planets, and accounts for the growth and reproduction of living things, the instinct and tendencies of animals, the work of bees, the nest-building of birds, the activity of the mind of man?

**The laws of Nature have been imposed by a lawgiver.**—

(1) The arguments by which we have shown that the laws of nature are not due to chance avail, also, to prove that those laws cannot be due to any unintelligent cause we choose to name. Therefore, they must be due to some great intelligence distinct from matter. They must have been ordained and imposed by a Lawgiver. And, as the statesman frames his legislation for a

---

[2] Order is unity, or uniformity, amid variety. Examples: (1) The human body consists of a great number of members and organs, yet all help, each in its own way, towards the well-being of the whole. (2) Matter attracts matter. Bodies may vary considerably in mass. They may be as large as a planet, or as small as a speck of dust, yet all act in the same way. Amid a great variety of masses, there is uniformity of action. Order is the result of design. Design may, therefore, be defined as the planning of order.

[3] We abstract for the moment from the rare interpositions to which, according to the doctrine of miracles, the laws of nature are subject

definite purpose. so, also, the Lawgiver of the universe imposed His laws to achieve the ends He desired. The orderly arrangement produced by His laws was intentional. It was in accordance with His preconceived plan or design.

(2) Observe how the necessity for an intelligent author of the laws of nature is enforced by considerations such as the following:

(*a*) Great intelligence and skilful workmanship are required to construct a steam-engine that can feed itself with fuel and water. But indefinitely greater would be the intelligence and power which could make the iron-ore come of itself out of the bowels of the earth, smelt and temper itself, form and fit together all the parts of the engine, make the engine lay in its store of water and coal, kindle its furnace, and repair its worn parts. Yet this is an everyday process of nature in the case of living organisms. And as intelligence is needed to guide the hands of the mechanic who builds the engine, much more is it needed to combine and direct the lifeless forces of nature in producing more marvellous results.

(*b*) The worker-bees construct their cells so as to give a maximum of strength and capacity with a minimum of material, thereby solving practically a problem in advanced mathematics.[4] They get their knowledge neither by reasoning nor from instruction, for all possess it at the moment of maturity. They do not get it by heredity, for their parents, the queens and the drones, build no cells. Whence, then, did they derive it? Manifestly from some distinct intelligence, from some Being who knew how the problem should be solved, and who implanted in them as a law of their nature the necessary impulse to accomplish their allotted task.[5] For another example of instinct, see Ch. II., footnote [4].

(*c*) Man is as much a product of nature as the bee or the flower. The elaborate works of civilization, the arts and sciences, and all the accumulated knowledge of centuries, are as certainly due to the working of nature's laws or forces, as the honey-cell of the bee or the perfume of the flower. Is it for a moment conceivable

---

[4] The problem was proposed to König by Réaumur in the following form: "To find the construction of a hexagonal prism terminated by a pyramid composed of three equal and similar rhombs, such that the solid may be made of the least quantity of materials." König found the angles of the rhombs to be 109° 26′ and 70° 34′, which result was slightly incorrect, the error being due to the table of logarithms which he used. It was afterwards discovered that the true values, correctly found by the bees, are 109° 28′ and 70° 32′. See Encyc. Brit. vol. iii., pp. 490, 484, 9th ed.

[5] If, against all likelihood, it should ever be proved that the insects act from individual intelligence, the question would still remain to be put: How have they come to possess that intelligence, and why is it specially adapted to their work?

that those laws were not directed by intelligence, that man and all his achievements could have sprung from a source, blind and lifeless, and, therefore, totally inadequate to account for them?

**The lawgiver is God.**—(1) As the carpenter is distinct from the table he makes, the architect from the house he designs, as every cause is distinct from its effect, so the Lawgiver of the universe must be distinct from the universe and its laws. (2) A scientist of exceptional talent, aided by perfect apparatus for research, succeeds after many years of study in understanding, more or less imperfectly, the working of one or two of those laws. Must not, then, the Author of them all be a Being of vast intelligence? (3) That Being must possess free-will. Else, how does man by a law of his nature come to possess such a faculty? And why should the laws of nature be precisely as they are—we see no reason why they might not be otherwise—except from the act of a Being free to choose as He pleases? (4) But is that Being the First Cause? May He not Himself be the creature of another, that other of a third, and so on without end? No. Such a series is unthinkable. It must ultimately depend on some one being. That Being would be God, the First Cause, Intelligent and Free.

**Objection (1)—The laws of nature may be due to blind forces inherent in matter itself.**—We are here dealing with Materialist Evolution. We may express the doctrine in the following form: "Nothing exists, nothing ever existed, but matter, *i.e.*, nothing but what has extension, and can be perceived by the senses. The universe was once a fiery rotating nebula. Its molecules possessed those chemical and physical forces which, by action and interaction, have gradually evolved the great variety of things, with and without life, which we see in the world at the present day. Living creatures are, therefore, nothing more than cunning clocks. Thought and will are mere motions of matter." Criticism: (*a*) If nothing exists but matter, then this theory itself does not exist, for it is imperceptible to the senses. (*b*) Whence did the nebula derive its motion, and its molecules their physical and chemical forces? They always had them, say the evolutionists. Motion, they assert, is, and has always been, inherent in eternally existing matter. But "inherent motion" is an absurdity. Matter of all kinds is indifferent to motion or rest. This truth, admitted by all physicists, is expressed in Newton's Laws of Motion. Moreover, motion must be in some particular direction, and the direction must be determined by a cause distinct from the body moved. As regards the laws which the atoms of matter obey, why do all atoms of the same kind obey the same laws? Why, for instance, do the atoms of hydrogen in a distant star, as the spectroscope tells us, obey the same laws as the hydrogen we prepare in our chemical laboratories?—We show in our Note on the Dissipation of Energy that the particular forms of motion which we find in the world at the present day had a beginning, and will have an end. (*c*) The theory assumes quite gratuitously the possibility of the origin of life from non-living matter.[5a] As the science of Biology advances, that possibility is being more and more discounted. It has been demonstrated that the living cell possesses a structure complicated beyond description, and that, in its action, it differs essentially from any machine that we know of.[6] (*d*) Even though the great chasm between living and lifeless matter were successfully bridged, there would still remain the greater chasms between sentient and non-sentient life, thinking and non-thinking. (*e*) On a general survey, see what the theory proposes:—Inorganic matter, by some process which the modern chemist with all his knowledge cannot even conceive, produced of itself the first living thing; that living thing got, somehow or other, the power of propagating itself, and of developing, under a law of unexplained origin, into the higher forms of life, and finally into man himself: poets, philosophers, scientists, and all their works, are, therefore, the offspring of a mere clod of earth, developing under the influence of a law which sprang out of nowhere, which was imposed by no lawgiver, which wrought and shaped with consummate skill, although there was not a glimmer of intelligence to guide it. The more this Mechanical, or Materialist, Evolution is examined, the more preposterous it seems. It was much in vogue among non-Catholics during the latter years of the nineteenth century. It was advocated by Tyndall[7] (†1893) and others, as the full and final explanation of all things, but, nowadays, the difficulties against its acceptance are generally admitted to be overwhelming. Haeckel, however, has attempted to revitalize it.

He maintains that all matter is alive and endowed with sensation and will.[8] Needless to say, he produces not a particle of evidence

---

[5a] A remarkable illustration of the truth that life can come only from life is found in the modern aseptic treatment of wounds. This treatment depends on two facts, viz., (1) that, if germs are permitted to get into a wound, they may propagate their kind, and so cause putrefaction, often with fatal results to the patient; (2) that, if germs be entirely excluded from the wound, no corruption takes place, and the healing process is unimpeded.

[6] See Windle, *The Church and Science*, c. xxv., where authorities are quoted.

[7] Belfast Address; Collected Essays.—The mark † denotes date of death.

[8] *Riddle of the Universe*, pp. 46, 64, 78. Scientists look with suspicion on much of Haeckel's work, as he has been convicted of inventing and distorting evidence.

for his contention, which, moreover, is rejected by all physicists as utterly baseless.[9] Even though admitted, it would be no sufficient explanation of the evolution of the world. (a) The "will" which he ascribes to primal matter is, on his own admission, nothing but the "tendency to avoid strain," and "sensation," nothing better than an extremely attenuated and rudimentary power of perception. "Will" which is not will, and "sensation" which is far beneath the humblest sense-power within our knowledge could not, of themselves, by any possibility account for the freewill of which we are all conscious, for the great products of the human intellect, and for the entire order of the world. It is a maxim in philosophy, approved by common sense, that, without extrinsic aid, the less can never produce the greater: life, therefore, cannot come from dead matter, nor sentient life from the non-sentient, nor rational life from the irrational, except by the act of some Power capable of breathing into matter these higher activities. (b) Physicists admit that the universe is bound together in a close unity, and that every particle of matter affects, and is affected by, every other. To account satisfactorily for the existing order of the universe on the lines of Haeckel, each particle of matter should be capable of understanding the whole plan, and its own particular and ever-changing, part in it. It should, moreover, be willing constantly to co-operate with every other particle. In such a supposition, which is not advanced by anyone, every particle of matter would be God. But the question whether God is one or many does not concern us at this stage of our argument. Further on we prove that God must be one. (c) Even if it could be proved that the world has passed through an orderly and progressive development, like the seed that becomes a giant of the forest, then the argument for the necessity of a designer, lawgiver, and perfecter, so far from losing force, would but receive an intensified cogency.[10]

**Objection (2)—The sufferings of life and the prodigality of Nature seem to argue against the wisdom of God:**—We cannot hope to understand God's purpose in everything. His design is not always clear to us. (a) Sometimes we not only fail to discover wisdom in the happenings of life, but seem to find a colossal cruelty in them. "Why," we ask, "is there so much pain and grief in the world?" But, if there were no pain nor grief, there would be no pity nor self-sacrifice, no noble discipline for the soul

---

[9] For a full refutation of Haeckel, see Fr. Gerard's, *The Old Riddle and the Newest Answer*, Longmans, Green, price 7d.
[10] We return to the theory of Evolution, Part II., The Creation.

of man. To complete our answer we must look to Revelation. It will tell us of the fall of man and its consequences.[10a]

(b) Sometimes we marvel at the prodigality of Nature, and ask ourselves why there are so many useless things in the world. On this point St. George Mivart says that if the animals called labyrinthodonts which belong to the early geological ages had been endowed with intelligence, they might have made a strong case against the wisdom of Providence from the lavish waste of fern spores. Yet, all that vegetable waste has given us our coal. The animals would have judged wrongly "from their not being able to foresee events of what was to them an incalculably remote future. . . . Let a brood of young birds die before fledging," he continues, "their bodies feed a multitude of smaller creatures, these serve for others; and ultimately swarms of bacteria reduce lifeless organic matter to elements which serve to nourish vegetation, which serves to feed worms and other creatures, which again actively minister to the welfare of all the higher animals and of man. Nature is so arranged that the purpose of its First Cause can never be defeated, happen what may."[11] We may add that our argument does not require us to prove design in *all* things. It is sufficient to prove it in *some* things. Neither are we called on to prove that the design is perfect. Whether perfect or imperfect, it establishes the existence of a Designer: a hand-loom proves the existence of a designer just as well as a loom driven by steam, although the design may be less perfect in the one case than in the other.

**Note.—The Dissipation of Energy.** ALL USEFUL ENERGY IS BEING CONVERTED INTO UNIFORMLY DIFFUSED HEAT.—Every student of physical science knows that a portion of the energy employed in doing work appears as heat which tends to diffuse itself uniformly. The amount of energy converted into diffused heat is constantly increasing, and, as no useful work can be extracted from it (II. Law of Thermodynamics), it is justly described as the growing waste-heap of the universe. Even if the sum of energy in the universe be constant, the amount available for useful work is continually diminishing. The universe, therefore, is tending to a state of rest in which all useful work, and, hence, all life, such as we know it, will be impossible.[12]

WHEREFORE, IT FOLLOWS THAT THE USEFUL ENERGY OF THE UNIVERSE HAD A BEGINNING.—With Lord Kelvin, we may compare the universe to a lighted candle: "regarding the universe," he says,

---
[10a] See Part II., Ch. VII.
[11] *Nature and Thought*, 1885 : p. 218.
[12] See points 2 and 3, note on Argt. from Contingence.

"as a candle that has been lit, we become absolutely certain that it has not been burning from eternity, and that a time must come when it will cease to burn." Or, we may compare it to a clock which is going. The movement of the clock is due to a spring slowly uncoiling. There is no mechanism within the clock to rewind the spring. At some point in the future it will stop. At some point in the past it was wound up by the hand of man or by some agency distinct from itself. It is so with the universe. As surely as the springs of its energy approach at every instant the final stage of complete relaxation, so surely were they, at some moment in the past, wound up by some extrinsic agency, by the hand of God.[13]

## II. Argument from the Universal Belief of Mankind.

### § 1.—*Brief treatment.*

All nations in every age have agreed in proclaiming the existence of some Divine Power presiding over the world. Such an agreement, so universal, so persistent amid such a diversity of circumstances and persons, could have been produced only by some one, universal, and persistently active, cause. That cause is none other than the natural use of human reason itself. The reason of mankind, therefore, has arrived at the conclusion that the only satisfactory explanation of the world and its marvels, and of man himself, is to be found in the existence of some great Living Force, some Divine Power, the Creator of all things. The reason of mankind cannot argue falsely. Were we to make such a supposition, we should infer that human reason tends naturally to error.

---

[13] This argument is a direct deduction from established physical laws: see Preston's *Heat*, 296-298. Addressed to materialists, it is an *argumentum ad hominem*, i.e., an argument based on their own admissions. They, in common with all physicists, regard the laws of energy as the very foundation of physical science. It has been suggested that there may be a means in nature for the sudden restoration of useful energy (*cataclysmic theory*). But this is merely a gratuitous assumption, unsupported by scientific evidence.

In other words, we should have to admit that the discovery of truth is impossible.

*Objections.*

(1) " Science has disproved the belief, once universal, that the sun moves round the earth, and may, likewise, some day disprove the belief in the existence of God."—Reply: Physical science has, indeed, corrected many errors, once widely prevalent, and may prove, as it advances, that theories, now firmly held by scientists themselves, are as false as the astronomy of the ancients. But the progress of science can never touch the belief in the existence of God. Science is restricted to examining the mechanism of the visible world. It is restricted to showing how one movement or change is generated by another. But how the world originated, and how its motion began—these are questions that lie entirely beyond its scope. The scientist is like a man who examines the works of a clock, and shows how this wheel is moved by that, but who never inquires as to the hand that made the timepiece and set it going. Further, owing to inexact observation and hasty inference, there is always room for error in our speculations as to the physical causes of natural events, but there is no room for error in the reasoning that underlies the universal belief in God. That belief is based on arguments too clear and simple ever to be overthrown, such, *e.g.*, as the following :—" Design is plainly visible in the world, and design proves the existence of a Designer "; " the world is an inanimate thing; it cannot account for its existence; it must have been made by a Being distinct from it."

(2) " The belief is of no value, since some men say that there is one God, others that there are many Gods." Reply: For our argument, it is unnecessary that all men should agree as to whether God is one or many. The proof that He exists is simple, hence the universal agreement. The proof that He is one is difficult, hence the errors as to His nature.

## § 2.—*Fuller treatment.*

**There is, and there has always been, a universal belief in the existence of a Divine Power presiding over the world.**—The belief in the existence of some Divine Power presiding over the world has prevailed at all times and among all nations in spite of wide differences in customs, civilization, and ideals. Ample testimony to the truth of this assertion will be found in the works of ancient writers and modern ethnologists. (1) Ancient writers:— *e.g.*, Cicero (1st century B.C.): "there is no nation so wild and fierce as not to know that it must have a god, although it may not know what sort of god it should be, *De Leg.*, 1, 8; Plutarch (1st cent. A.D.), "if you go round the world, you may find cities without walls, or literature, or kings, or houses, or wealth, or money, without gymnasia or theatres. But no one ever saw a city without temples and gods," Adv. Colot. Epic, 31, 5; Clement of Alexandria and many others in the early ages of the Church. (2) Modern ethnologists:—*e.g.*, Peschel, "to the question which we now ask whether, anywhere in the world, a tribe has been found, destitute of all religious impulses and ideas, we must reply with a decided negative," Völkerkunde, 1885, p. 273; Max Müller, who says of this proof that not only has it never been refuted but that it renders all other proofs for the existence of God unnecessary, Anthrop. Religion, 1894, p. 90. It was thought at one time that there were some few tribes with no religious ideas, but it has been found that this opinion originated either in imperfect investigation or in the reluctance of some uncivilized peoples to speak of their beliefs to strangers. Among educated people there are some who profess atheism, but they are so few as to be negligible.[14] Probably they are not more numerous than those learned men who set themselves against the common sense of the human race by maintaining, *e.g.*, that the external world does not exist, that nothing exists but their own perceptions, or by holding that, in some other planet, a straight line may not be the shortest distance between two points.

**This belief is the expression of the collective reason of humanity, and must, therefore, be true.**—The belief in the existence of a Divine Power, so universal, so persistent amid such a vast diversity of circumstances and persons, could have been produced only by some universal and persistently active cause. That cause must be found in the natural use of the human reason, drawing its conclusion from the existence of the world, from the marvels of nature, and from the promptings of the human heart.

---

[14] See below, Atheism.

We admit that our reason errs at times, and we may grant without hesitation that the reason of many men, or rather the abuse of their reason, particularly when they live together and are influenced by like considerations, may lead them to the same erroneous conclusion: but we must regard it as quite inconceivable that the reason of all men in all ages could have forced them into the same conclusion, identical and erroneous.[15] Were we to make such an admission, we should at once be compelled to lose all trust in human reason and to confess that the discovery of truth is impossible. We must, therefore, hold the universal belief in the existence of a Divine Power to be true, because it is the expression of the collective reason of humanity, the voice of nature itself.[16]

**Objection** (1) "There was at one time a universal belief that the sun went round the earth, but the belief proved to be false. The same fate may some day befall the belief in the existence of a Divine Power." Reply:—The error as to the relation of the sun to the earth arose from a too hasty inference. The sense of sight and the other senses are trustworthy only in regard to their own proper work. The eye can tell us only of appearances. It can tell us that an object appears to move, but we must depend on our reason to ascertain whether the appearance of motion is due to motion in the object or to motion in ourselves. But there is no source of error in the reasoning which underlies the belief in the existence of a Divine Power. That belief is based on such arguments as the following:—"Design is plainly visible in the world, and design proves the existence of a Designer," "the world is an inanimate thing; it cannot account for its existence; it must have been made by some Being distinct from it." Universal error in such simple reasoning is inconceivable. Further, as we show in replying to the next objection, no advance in science can ever dispense with the necessity for some Living Force distinct from the world.

**Objection** (2) "The universal belief may have arisen from ignorance of natural causes. Men in early times, not being able to

---

[15] See below, replies to Objections (1) and (2).

[16] We must trust human reason as we trust our senses. An individual may err, but mankind cannot err. An individual may suffer from some defect of mind or body, and may, therefore, err in his reasoning, or in his perception of colour, shape, sound, etc. He discovers his error by comparing his reasoning or his perception with the reasoning or perception of the rest of mankind. We may put the entire argument in this form:—normal human reason is right in its conclusions; normal human reason is the reason of mankind generally; the reason of mankind generally has arrived at the conclusion that God exists; therefore, that conclusion must be true.

discover the physical causes of lightning, rain, the growth of plants and animals, attributed them to a Divine Power." Reply:—The objection rests on the fallacy that an effect is fully explained by its physical cause. A physical cause is a cause whose operation comes under the observation of the senses. We will show by an example that it is never the complete explanation of its effect. Suppose we are asked to account for the letters we see in this printed page. The physical causes of those letters are the metal type, the ink, the absorbent nature of the paper, the printer's hands and eyes. But, clearly, these causes do not explain how the page came to be printed. The real cause is not physical. It is the free-will of the printer. Note how the example applies to the motion we observe in the world around us: the physicist explains the motion of the train by the motion in the piston of the engine; the motion in the piston by the expansion of steam; the expansion of the steam by the heat from the coal; the energy in the coal, which is nothing more than compressed vegetable matter, by the sun's heat and light; the sun's heat and light by the motion of the nebula out of which it was evolved. Therefore, as far as a complete explanation is concerned, we find ourselves, at the end of the long series of physical causes, just where we were at the beginning. The motion of the nebula requires explanation just as much as the motion of the train. The objection, therefore, does not tell against us in the least. Rather, it directs our attention to the right reason of man which finds the ultimate explanation of all physical phenomena in the will of some all-powerful Being distinct from the world.[16a]

**Objection** (8) "Might not the belief have sprung from fear? Might not fear of the stupendous forces of nature, the lightning, the thunder, the earthquake, the volcano, have led to their personification?" Reply:—Fear might emphasize the belief in God but

---

[16a] We may bring out the point of this argument by means of a humorous illustration used for a somewhat different purpose by W. G. Ward in his work, *The Philosophy of Theism*, vol. ii., p. 173. He supposes a "philosophical" mouse to be enclosed in a pianoforte. The mouse discovers that every sound of the instrument is produced by a vibration of the strings, and the vibration of the strings by taps of the hammers. "Thus far I have already prosecuted my researches," says the mouse. And he goes on with all the blithe optimism of the Atheist: "So much is evident even now, viz., that the sounds proceed not . . . from any external agency, but from the uniform operation of fixed laws. These laws may be explored by intelligent mice; and to their exploration I shall devote my life." And so, the mouse, arguing himself out of the old belief of his kind, becomes convinced that the piano-player has no existence.

could not create it. If the objection were sound, a man's progress in the knowledge of physical science should be accompanied by decay in his religious belief. But this is not the case. On the contrary, the greatest minds among scientists acknowledge the necessity for an Intelligent Author of the world.[17]

**Objection** (4) "The belief may have been encouraged by priests and lawgivers or kings; by priests who sought private gain in the deception of the people; by lawgivers, who wished to secure respect for their enactments by the threat of Divine chastisement." Reply:—A deception of the kind might be successful in this country or that, and for a short time, but surely not everywhere and continuously. The belief has been fostered by priests and rulers, no doubt, but that process has been made possible only by the fact that the belief was always welling up in the human heart. False beliefs without number have been taught, and enforced even with the sword, but have followed their authors to the tomb. This belief alone appears to have an unfailing vitality.

**Objection** (5) "The belief is of no value since men are not at one on the question of the Divine Nature. Some say there is but one God, others say that there are many." Reply:—For our argument, it is unnecessary that men should agree as to the nature of God, whether He is one or many. It is sufficient that underlying the beliefs of all men there is this identical substratum of agreement—viz., that the world is under the government of some Divine Power. The proof that a Divine Power exists is simple, hence universal agreement. The proof that He is one is difficult, hence the errors as to His nature.

**Objection** (6) "The belief may be nothing more than the blurred memory of a revelation which the ancestors of the human race fancied they had received from God." Reply:—The survival of that ancient tradition over such a long tract of centuries, amid such an infinite diversity of circumstances, cannot be explained satisfactorily, unless we hold that, at all times and in all lands, human reason was leading men to belief in God's existence.

### III. Argument from the Origin of Mind.

In man, there are two distinct things, mind and matter. All matter, in the natural world, has extension: it has a definite length, breadth, and thickness. Mind has no ex-

---

[17] See below, Atheism.

## THE EXISTENCE OF GOD.

tension. It is a power of acting in a particular way, and is imperceptible to the senses. A man's mind can conceive abstract ideas, such as "beauty," "goodness," etc. It can reason, *i.e.*, it can pass, as in the study of geometry, from truths already established to others not previously known. It possesses free-will, *i.e.*, it has the power of self-direction. Now, such concepts as "beauty" and "goodness" are not material things. They cannot be grasped by mere matter. Nor can we conceive mere matter to be capable of passing from one truth to another. Least of all can we conceive mere matter to have the power of directing itself. Matter moves only as it is moved. Its motion, and the direction of its motion, come from without. But, the mind of man can move itself in any direction it pleases. The mind of man, therefore, is what we term a spiritual thing, *i.e.*, it can act independently of, and is utterly different from, matter. If it is impossible to make a cube out of squares, it is, so to speak, even more impossible to make mind out of matter.

There was a time, as scientists tell us, when no living thing, neither plant, animal, nor man existed in the world.[18] There was a time, therefore, when nothing existed but inert matter. How, then, did mind begin to be? It cannot have made itself, for self-creation is a mere absurdity. It cannot have sprung from matter, for matter possesses in no form whatsoever the properties of mind. It must, therefore, have been made by some Being, capable of calling things into existence at His word, and endowed like itself, but in an infinitely higher way, with intelligence and free-will. That Being is God.

(For the detailed proof of the Spirituality of the Soul see Ch. II.)

---

[18] Observe, the validity of our argument is not affected in the least by the contention, unwarranted, as we show in Ch. II., that the lower animals possess intelligence.

## IV. Argument from Contingence.

### § 1.—*Brief treatment.*

Everything in the visible world is subject to change and death. Plants, animals, and men come into being, and after a short time perish, while inanimate matter suffers endless changes. No particular thing in the universe has any grip on existence: existence is no part of its nature. Everything in the world, therefore, is contingent, *i.e.*, it does not exist of itself, but is dependent on something else for its existence.

Since contingent beings do, as a fact, exist, they must be held in existence by a self-existent being, *i.e.*, by a being to whose nature existence belongs. Can the self-existent being be mere matter, modifying itself in various ways? No; matter cannot account for the laws of nature, the origin of life, sensation, and the spiritual and free soul of man. The self-existent being must be a living, personal being. It is only such a one that can account satisfactorily for the universe and all its marvels.

### § 2.—*Fuller treatment.*

**Everything in the visible world is contingent.**—The world in which we live is constantly changing. Plants, animals, and men appear and disappear, and inanimate matter passes through endless variations.[19] We may accept the word of scientists that what we see around us to-day is one of a long series of changes which began when the earth was part of a fiery nebula. Birth and death—using the words in the broad sense of coming into, and passing

---

[19] Consider, *e.g.*, our planet alone: (1) the distribution of land and water is insensibly, but constantly, changing; (2) the earth's rotatory motion is getting slower and slower, because the tide, the great bank of water piled up by the attraction of the moon, acts as a brake on it; (3) the motion of the earth round the sun is also being retarded, because of friction with clouds of meteoric dust: the earth is, therefore, ever being drawn closer to the sun. Enormous changes will result, after the lapse of ages, as a consequence of (2) and (3).

out of, existence—is a universal law to which all things, living and lifeless, are subject. Nothing in the world, therefore, has any grip, as it were, on existence. Nothing in the world exists necessarily. If we were asked to set down all those things which constitute a man, *e.g.*, we should not mention "existence" as one of them, for we know that man need not exist. The same holds of any other particular thing in the visible world we choose to name. We say, therefore, that everything in the visible world is contingent, *i.e.*, that existence is no part of its nature, but that it must depend for its existence on something outside itself.[19a]

**Contingent beings require for their support a self-existent being.**—If things which need not exist do exist, as a fact, they must have been brought into existence and must be held in existence by something distinct from them. This "something" must exist necessarily, *i.e.*, existence must be part of its nature. For, if it did not exist necessarily, it would itself require ultimately the support of something necessarily existing, otherwise we should find ourselves in the position of the Indians who said that the world was supported by an elephant, the elephant by a tortoise, and the tortoise by nothing. We must, therefore, hold that the world is kept in existence by a necessary or self-existent being, a being that contains within itself the source of its own existence.

**The self-existent being is God.**—Is the self-existent being nothing more than basic matter, modifying itself in various ways, and producing the particular things that flit into and out of existence? No, for the effects must be within the capacity of the cause. Matter, as we have seen, cannot account for the laws of nature and all the wonders that result from them; it cannot account for the origin of life, the origin of sensation, the origin of the spiritual and free soul of man. These things can be accounted for only by ascribing them to a self-existent being endowed with intelligence and free-will. And as to matter itself, it cannot account for its own existence. Its existence must be attributed to the same self-existent being, for He who created the human soul could have, and must have, created matter also. The self-existent being is God, the First Cause, Intelligent and Free, the Creator of all things outside Himself. He made them by an act of His will,

---

[19a] We claim that each *particular* thing in the visible world is contingent. We do not claim that matter itself—basic matter—is contingent. We do not know enough about basic matter to assert at once that it is contingent, "because it can be conceived as non existing."

## THE EXISTENCE OF GOD.

and by His will He sustains them in being. Of themselves they have no hold on existence, for existence is no part of their nature. Their existence from instant to instant is the gift of His Goodness to them, and may be withdrawn at His pleasure.[20]

(—*See Supplementary Notes, p.* 138.)

## THE NATURE OF GOD.

We may arrive at some knowledge of the Nature of God from the fact that He is the First Cause, eternal, self existent. Our deductions, however, must appear cold and formal to those who have been taught by Bethlehem and Calvary to know God and to love Him with a warm personal love. The Incarnation of the Son of God has given mankind an infinitely clearer idea of the Divine Nature than all the reasoning of philosophy.

**Simplicity.**—God must be simple, *i.e.*, He cannot consist of separate parts united into one whole. In a being so compounded, it is the union of parts that forms the whole. This union would require a cause. But the First Cause is uncaused.

**Spirituality.**—God cannot be matter, because all matter is made up of parts. He is, therefore, a being with no extension. But He is also an active, intelligent being, because He is the Creator of all things, including the human soul. An active, intelligent, being without extension is a spirit. Therefore, God is a spirit.

**Infinity.**—God is infinite, *i.e.*, every perfection that can exist belongs to him.

A. We speak of a living plant, a living animal, a living man. Each of these possesses but a share of life, a limited life. But, suppose that there was such a thing as "Life Itself" actually existing. It would not be a mere share of life, a limited life. It would be Perfect Life. Now, apply this to what we know of

---

[20] More abstruse arguments for the Existence of God will be found in St. Thomas, *Summa Theologiae*, and *Summa Contra Gentiles*. Of the simpler and more accessible works on the subject, the following should be read:—*The Existence of God*, Canon Moyes, D.D.: Sands, price 7d.; *The Old Riddle and the Newest Answer*, Fr. Gerard, S.J.: Longmans, Green, price 7d.; *The Existence of God : a Dialogue*, Fr. Clarke, S.J.: C.T.S., price 7d.—(the reference to the human eye, p. 18, should be corrected by note 2, p. 34, of Fr. Gerard's work referred to above); *The World and its Maker*, Fr. Gerard, S.J.: C.T.S., price 4d.

God's existence. He exists necessarily. He never began to exist. He can never cease existing. We must, therefore, identify Him with Existence Itself, for it is only Existence Itself that can never be conceived as non-existing. All other things get a share of existence from Him. Their existence is limited. He is Existence Itself. He must, therefore, be Perfect Existence.

B. (1) We speak of men as possessing various perfections, *e.g.*, wisdom, justice, courage, reasoning power, but not as possessing them in a perfect degree. No man is perfectly wise, just, courageous, logical. May we predicate all these things of God? No, not all, since some of them involve an imperfection. We may say that God is perfectly wise, *i.e.*, that He knows the causes of all things, or that He is perfectly just, *i.e.*, that He rewards and punishes according to merit. But we cannot say that He is perfectly courageous, for courage implies a willingness to face danger, and danger implies weakness, a condition in which one's life is threatened. Neither can we say that He is perfectly logical, for the epithet implies the power of passing from the known to the unknown, and to God nothing can be unknown.

(2) The perfections, traces of which we observe in men, are, therefore, of two kinds, absolute and relative. Absolute perfections of their own nature involve no imperfection, while relative perfections do involve an imperfection. The former class God possesses *formally*—that is, He possesses them as they are in themselves. The latter class He possesses *eminently*—that is, He is the source, perfect in itself, whence they are derived.

(3) Agnostics [21] say that the perfections we ascribe to God are merely "anthropomorphic," *i.e.*, imitations of human perfections; that if, for instance, a watch could think, it would have just as much right to argue that the watchmaker was made up of springs and cog-wheels, as we have to say that God possesses intelligence, goodness, justice, etc. We reply (*a*) that we do not ascribe to God mere imitations of our human perfections; that the perfections we ascribe to God are found in Him in an infinitely higher manner than in creatures; that in creatures intelligence, goodness, justice are distinct qualities, while in God, in some incomprehensible way, they and all perfections are one and the same, identical with His nature or essence; (*b*) that, if the analogy of the watch were justified, we should be found ascribing to God hands and eyes and bodily organs, but such is not the fact; that, if the watch could reason aright, it would justly ascribe to the watchmaker the beginning of its movement and the orderly arrangement of its parts.

---

[21] See below, Atheism.

## THE EXISTENCE OF GOD.

**Unity.**—(1) Since God is infinite, He must be One. Two infinite beings, each containing all perfections that can possibly exist, would be a contradiction. If there were two infinite beings, each should possess some perfection which the other had not, otherwise they would not be distinct. But since each would be infinite, each should possess all perfections. Moreover, each would be independent, and outside the power of the other. Hence, neither could be infinite.

(2) Since God is Existence Itself, He must be One, for Existence Itself is one. If there were two Gods, each would possess but a share of existence, and neither would be identical with Existence Itself.

**Omnipotence.**—God is omnipotent because He is infinite. All things that are possible He can do. They are possible only because He can do them. They can come into existence only because He can bring them into existence. He cannot contradict His own Will or Truth. He cannot commit sin, for instance, for the essence of sin is opposition to His Will. Nor can He attempt what is absurd, the making, for instance, of a four-sided triangle. Such a figure would be a mere nothing, a contradiction in terms. Men, because of the imperfection of their will or understanding, commit sin, or undertake what is intrinsically absurd.

**Omnipresence and Omniscience.**—God is everywhere, for He supports in existence everything outside Himself. He is Omniscient, that is, He knows all things. He is Omniscient because His knowledge is infinite. He has not a number of distinct ideas as we have. By one act of His intellect He knows and knew from all eternity all things past, present, and to come.

**Note.**—The Nature of God is incomprehensible. But so is our own nature. So is the nature of all things around us from the star to the daisy by the wayside. Sir Isaac Newton, one of the greatest scientists that ever lived, compared himself to a little child picking up a few shells on the shore, while all the depths of the ocean remained hidden from him. He felt that his momentous discoveries had revealed, but without explaining, just one or two levers in the infinitely complicated structure of the universe, while all the rest lay beyond in impenetrable darkness. His knowledge seemed to him as nothing compared with his ignorance. If it be so difficult, then, to know anything worth knowing of the visible world, how incomparably more difficult it must be to understand the Nature of its Author?

## ATHEISM.

We apply the term "atheist," not to those who deny the existence of an Ultimate Reality, a First Cause of all things, for there are none such, but to those who deny the existence of a Personal God, Intelligent and Free, to whom men are responsible for their actions.

(1) The fact that the greatest minds in all ages were firm believers in a Personal God refutes the contention that such a belief is the mark of ignorance and low civilization. Our belief, and the belief of the vast majority of mankind, was the belief (a) of the ancient philosophers, Socrates, Plato, and Aristotle, men to whom the modern world owes a debt that cannot easily be estimated; (b) of the astronomers, Copernicus, Galileo, Kepler, Newton, Leverrier, and Herschel; of the chemists, Berzelius, Dumas, Liebig, Chevreul, Davy, and Dalton; of the zoologist and geologist, Cuvier; of Schwann, the founder of the modern school of physiology; of the physicists, Ohm, Ampère, Galvani, Volta, Faraday, Joule, Clerk Maxwell, and Lord Kelvin; and of Pasteur, to whom humanity is so much indebted for having founded the study of bacteriology.[22] These are but a few of the names that might be mentioned. An exhaustive list would include the greatest statesmen, artists, poets, generals, inventors and scholars of every age.

(2) Atheism is found chiefly among (a) men who find the belief in a Personal God an irksome check on the indulgence of their passions,[23] and (b) students of physical science who from a too intense concentration on their own particular line of work come to doubt all that is spiritual and moral, everything in fact except those things to which the tests of the laboratory can be applied.[23a]

Atheism has taken several forms, of which the following are the chief:—

**Materialism.**—In ancient times the chief materialists were Democritus of Abdēra (†360 B.C.), and Epicurus (†270 B.C.); in modern times, the French Encyclopaedists (Diderot and D'Alembert, c.[23b] 1750), Feuerbach († 1872), Moleschott († 1893), Tyndall († 1893), and E. Haeckel. Materialists hold that nothing exists but matter and its modifications. We have refuted their doctrine in Arguments I., III., and IV. above.

---

[22] For a much fuller list, see A. Kneller, *Christianity and the Leaders of Modern Science.*

[23] "Keep your soul," says Rousseau, "always in a condition in which it will desire that there is a God, and you will never doubt His existence," Emile IV.

[23a] See Newman, *Idea of a University*, Disc. III. 6.

[23b] The letter "c" prefixed to a date denotes an approximation.

## THE EXISTENCE OF GOD.

**Pantheism.**—The chief pantheists were, in ancient times, Heraclītus (c. 500 B.C.), and the Stoics (a school of philosophy founded c. 350 B.C.); in modern times Spinoza († 1677), Fichte († 1814), Hegel († 1831), Schelling († 1854). Pantheism, in the form in which it is commonly professed, is the direct opposite of Materialism. Materialism holds that nothing exists but matter; Pantheism, that nothing exists but spirit, God, the Absolute. Therefore, according to the Pantheists, all the phenomena of the universe, all contingent beings, are but manifestations of the Divine Nature; everything is one and the same. The logical issue of these principles is to remove all distinction between right and wrong, and to identify God with all sorts of different things—good and evil, living and lifeless, intelligent and unintelligent, present, past, and future. Pantheists do not shrink from such conclusions, and so set themselves in opposition to the common-sense of mankind : "Is it not ridiculous," says Fr. Boedder,[24] " to say that a cat is the same real being with the mouse which she devours, and with the dog that worries her, and that cat and dog alike are the same being with the master who restores peace between them? Is it not absurd to maintain that the criminal to be hanged is really the same being with the judge who pronounces sentence of death against him, and with the executioner who carries out this sentence? And who can accept the statement that the atheist is substantially the same being with God whose existence he denies, and whose name he blasphemes?" Briefly, Pantheism must be rejected—(1) because it is opposed to the infinite perfection of God : God cannot change; He cannot become greater or less; He cannot be identical with what is limited, whether it be matter or human intelligence; (2) because it is opposed to human consciousness, *i.e.*, to the knowledge which a man has of his own mind : every man is conscious of his individuality and of his free-will; every man knows as clearly as he can know anything that he is distinct from the world around him, and that his will is free; if he is deceived in either of these, there is an end of certainty, and all reasoning becomes futile; further, if his will is not free, he is no longer responsible for his acts, and cannot be punished or rewarded for them, a conclusion opposed to the normal reason of mankind, and, therefore, unsound.

**Agnosticism.**—The term "Agnostic" was invented by Huxley († 1895). According to Herbert Spencer († 1903), the chief exponent of Agnosticism, the final explanation of the world is to be found in " an infinite, eternal energy from which all things pro-

---

[24] Natural Theology, p. 114, 1891. See *Pantheism*, Matthews: C.T.S., price 1d.

ceed—the ultimate Reality transcending human thought." This ultimate Reality is "unknown and unknowable."—We agree with the Agnostics that the "ultimate Reality," whom we call God, transcends human thought, in the sense that we cannot know Him adequately, but not in the sense that we can know nothing about Him. The Agnostics themselves, although they describe Him as "unknown and unknowable," profess to know that He is "an infinite, eternal energy from which all things proceed." If they know so much about Him, it is difficult to see how they can describe Him as either "unknown" or "unknowable." If by "infinite, eternal energy" they mean "infinite, eternal activity," their difference with us may be a mere matter of words. But if they mean energy of a merely physical kind—and this seems to be their meaning—then, they ascribe all the happenings of the world to motion of matter, and their position is that of the Materialists whom we have already refuted.[25]

**A general argument against Atheism.**—We have given the arguments against particular forms of Atheism. Against Atheism in general we urge the following consideration:—Society is necessary for man because it is only as a member of society that man can attain to the normal development of his faculties.[26] Society cannot exist unless its members observe the moral law. The mass of mankind will not observe the moral law unless they believe in a Personal God, All-powerful, All-knowing, who will reward the good and punish the wicked. Belief in a Personal God is, therefore, a demand of our very nature and must be true. It may be objected that there are atheists against whose lives nothing can be alleged. We reply that our statement refers to the mass of mankind, not to rare individuals; that good-living atheists are men who have been trained to habits of virtue by believing parents, and who have been surrounded from their birth by Christian influences; that Atheism, because it removes what is, practically, the only effective check on sin, tends of itself to moral degradation.

---

[25] The Agnostic practically rejects the use of inference as a means of arriving at truth. On its validity, see Introduction. See *Agnosticism*, Fr. Gerard, S.J.: C.T.S., price 1d.
[26] See Ch. III.

# CHAPTER II.

## THE HUMAN SOUL.

### A.

### THE SPIRITUALITY OF THE SOUL.

*Summary.*
> Meaning of life and soul.
> The soul gets its knowledge of material things through the senses of immaterial things through the mind.
> Man's will is free; how the will is exercised; definition of free-will.
> How man differs from the lower animals: man is progressive, because he is rational; the lower animals are stationary, because irrational; man's work is marked by diversity, because his will is free; the work of animals is marked by uniformity, because they are not free.
> Conclusion: the soul of man is spiritual, because it acts independently of matter and is self-directing. Therefore, it can exist apart from the body.

**The soul or principle of life.**—We are familiar with the common distinction between things with life and things without life. By life we understand a special kind of activity which manifests itself in various ways, in growth, sensation, free movement, intelligence and reasoning. Plants grow and put forth leaf and flower; animals feel pain or pleasure, and possess freedom of movement; man grows like the plant, he has feeling and movement like the animal, and, in addition, he thinks and reasons. Every living thing—plant, animal, or man—has within itself the source of its own activity. That source we call "soul" or "principle of life."[1] Now, just as, by reading of the behaviour of a man whom we have never seen, we may learn much about his character, so, without directly perceiving the soul, we may discover much about its nature by studying the acts that proceed from it.

**The human soul in relation to knowledge.**—Let us examine the activity of the human soul in relation to knowledge.

THE KNOWLEDGE GIVEN BY THE SENSES.—(a) Man is like a city with five gates through each of which messengers come with

---

[1] Strictly speaking, we may apply the word "soul" to the vital principle of plants and animals, but, in ordinary speech, we confine it to the vital principle of man.

tidings of what is passing in the outer world. These gates are the five senses, and each sense allows some special kind of knowledge to pass in. Man has no other means than these of knowing anything about the external world. Through the eye he gets a knowledge of colour, through the ear of sound, through the nose of smell, through the palate of taste, and through the whole surface of the body, but particularly through the hands, he comes to know of the resistance, hardness, and softness of bodies and such like. (b) The eye is the organ, or instrument, of sight, the ear of hearing, and so with the rest. Each organ is a part of the body, or, for the sense of touch, the entire body, and is acted on only by things that are themselves bodies—that is, by things that are material, things that have length, breadth, and thickness. The eye cannot see an object, unless its retina be set in motion by the vibrating ether; the ear cannot hear a sound, unless its tympanum be struck by the air-waves; the nostrils cannot perceive the perfume of a flower, unless the minute fragrant particles actually penetrate to them; the palate cannot taste, the hand cannot feel without coming into direct contact with their objects.

THE KNOWLEDGE GIVEN BY THE INTELLECT AND REASON.—(a) Man knows many more things than the senses tell him. Let us take some simple examples. We understand the meaning of such a word as "beauty," and yet we cannot have learned its import through the senses. We may have seen a beautiful landscape or statue, and we may have listened to a beautiful harmony, but "beauty" itself we have never seen, nor heard, nor grasped in any way by the senses. So, too, with such words as "truth," "goodness," "justice," and all other abstract terms. We may have heard a true statement, witnessed a good deed, listened to a just judgment, but "truth," "goodness," "justice" themselves we have never touched with any of the organs of sense. Again, take any of those terms which occur in geometry: a line, we are told, is length without breadth; a point is position merely, and has no parts or size. We understand such statements clearly, and yet we have never seen or felt, nor can we ever see or feel, geometrical lines or points. Or, further, take any common noun such as "man." No man that we ever saw was without a particular height, complexion, manner, and yet we think of none of these things when we use the word "man." We are thinking of something common to all men, but which, by itself, we have never seen or perceived by any of the senses. (b) The senses give us pictures, as it were, of the things in the outer world. Some power within us examines these pictures, and draws from them ideas and knowledge which the senses themselves could never have given us. That power we variously call intellect, reason, or mind. These are but other names for the thinking or rational soul.

**The activity of the soul in regard to free choice.**—MAN'S WILL IS FREE. Man is conscious that his will is free. Every day, in matters trivial or important, he exercises his freedom. When he chooses one course rather than another, he knows that he has acted freely and might have chosen differently. If he violate a law, the state will punish him, not exactly because he has violated it—for it will not punish him, if he be insane—but because he has violated it wilfully and was free to refrain from doing so. We chastise a dog for disobedience, not because we regard him as a free agent and as responsible for his act, but because we wish him to associate disobedience with suffering.

How FREE WILL IS EXERCISED. ITS DEFINITION.—(a) A man about to decide, let us suppose, whether he should study law or medicine, tries to take the measure of his aptitude for each of the two professions; he reckons up the years of preparation in each case, the means at his disposal, the chances of a successful career, and then, when he has fully deliberated, he decides—that is, he exercises his free will. So many points may not have to be considered in other cases, but the process is the same: there is first a deliberation, a weighing of advantages, and then a choice. But the choice is free. A man may select the lower instead of the higher advantage. (b) As the senses serve the intellect, so the intellect serves the will. It brings before the will, as before a master, the opposing advantages, and the will chooses between them. The advantages may be, and often are, of such a kind as to be manifestly imperceptible to the senses, *e.g.*, the advantages to the mind of studying astronomy rather than pure mathematics. Free-will may, therefore, be defined as *the power of choosing either of two courses represented as good by the intellect.* No man ever chooses evil as such. If he chooses what is, as a fact, evil, he chooses it in the belief, often blameworthy, that it is good, that it is serviceable to him in some way. Note that the intellect, in declaring a thing to be "good," sets it down as belonging to a large class of things. That class, to which the general name "good" is given, includes everything man can desire from mere bodily pleasure to the happiness of heaven and the vision of God Himself. "Good," therefore, cannot attract the senses, for it cannot be perceived by them. It *can* attract the will, for the will, like the intellect, has for its object things which are not matter.

**How man differs from the lower animals.**—MAN IS RATIONAL. THE LOWER ANIMALS ARE IRRATIONAL. Man has the faculty of reason, or the power of deducing new truths from those which he already knows, of passing from the known to the unknown. He is constantly pushing out the frontiers of knowledge; he adds new sciences to those already existing; he invents and perfects implements and machinery, rejecting the old for the new. The lower animals, on the other hand, are confined within the same circle of actions.[2] Bees are to day just as they were in the time of Moses and Aristotle; spiders, as they were in the days of the Pharaohs; birds build their nests now as they have always built them, in the same shape and with the same materials; the most sagacious of the lower animals, the horse and the dog, which have been in contact with man for countless centuries, exhibit not the slightest progress. The lower animals are not inventive.[3] They are held in a groove from which they cannot escape. They are stationary, because they are irrational. Man is progressive, because he is rational.[4]

---

[2] The variations due to change of habitat, etc., are negligible.

[3] This is universally admitted. The rudest implement, discovered deep down in the earth, is accepted by all as conclusive evidence of the work of man.

[4] Fabre, the chief authority on entomology, shows by many examples that the intelligence which insects exhibit does not reside in the insects themselves. Take the instance of the *ammophila hirsuta*. This insect, when preparing the worm as food for its larvae, cuts, as with a surgical lance, all its motor-nerve centres, so as to deprive it of movement, but not of life. The insect then lays its eggs beside the worm and covers all with clay. It has got its wonderful surgical skill without instruction or practice. It lives for but one season. It has not been taught by its parents, for it has never seen them. It does not teach its offspring, for it dies before they emerge from the earth. It has not got its skill by heredity. For, what does heredity mean in such a case? It means that some ancestor of the insect, having accidentally struck the worm in the nine or ten nerve centres, managed somehow or other to transmit to all its descendants a facility for achieving the same success. But it is mere folly to say that this chance act of the ancestor rather than any other chance act should become a fixed habit in all its progeny. And could the original success have been due to chance? Where the number of points that might have been struck was infinitely great, the chance of striking the nerve centres alone was zero. But, perhaps, the insect gets its skill by reasoning? No : (1) because reasoning does not give dexterity ; (2) because it is impossible that each insect of the same tribe—and all are equally expert—should discover by independent reasoning exactly the same process; (3) because, when the insect is confronted with the slightest novel difficulty, it acts like a creature without reason and is powerless to solve it. Therefore, the intelligence which the *ammophila* exhibits does not reside in the insect itself, but in the mind of the Designer who gave it the necessary impulse to fulfil its appointed task. (See Fabre, *Souvenirs Entomologiques, Duxième Série*, Delgrave, Paris).

## THE HUMAN SOUL.

**MAN IS FREE. THE LOWER ANIMALS ARE NOT.** Men apply their minds to an infinity of subjects, and pass from one occupation to another: a man may begin life as a labourer and end as an artist or a philosopher. The lower animals, on the other hand, are pinned down to one set of actions. They do not possess free-will; therefore, the characteristic of their work is uniformity.[5] Man does possess free-will; therefore, the characteristic of his work is diversity.[6]

**Conclusion; The Soul is Spiritual.**—The soul is spiritual, *i.e.*, it possesses activity, but has no extension and is utterly different from matter. (1) The soul is spiritual, because it acts independently of matter. It acts independently of matter, because it forms abstract and universal ideas, *e.g.*, " beauty," " goodness," " man," " triangle." Such ideas cannot be formed by the senses. They can be formed only by a faculty that resembles themselves in being immaterial. If the soul were a material thing and had extension like the senses, it could never pass beyond the pictures of concrete things with their definite shape, colour, hardness, etc. It could never deduce conclusions from known truths. It could never get a notion of God, or desire Him above all things in the visible world.

(2) The soul is spiritual, because it moves and directs itself, as it does in the exercise of free-will, while matter moves only as it is moved: matter gets its motion and the direction of its motion from without. While the soul is united to the body, the senses

---

[5] We admit, of course, that, in the same species of lower animals, some individuals behave more sagaciously than others, but such diversity is as nothing compared with the diversity we observe in the work of man.

[6] In the lower animals the absence of free will is a consequence of the fact that they are irrational. It may be objected that a hunting dog, *e.g.*, sometimes appears to deliberate and come to a decision as to which of two trails it is to follow. But the appearance of deliberation is due simply to the uncertainty of the animal as to which is the stronger trail. When the stronger trail is discovered, the dog follows it of necessity. The dog's action is determined from without. Man, on the other hand, in exercising free-will, determines himself. He may follow at pleasure the less instead of the greater advantage. Again, the dog's choice is a sensuous choice and must be distinguished from the intellectual choice of free-will. The free-will, even when exercised in choosing between different kinds of food, is acting on the information given it by the intellect. The intellect represents each of the two kinds of food as " good." " Good," however is a universal term like the word " man." It denotes a something which the senses cannot perceive. It belongs to the intellect alone—See *The Powers and Origin of the Soul*, and *Reason and Instinct*, by Fr. Northcote, C.T.S., price 1d each.

supply it with the materials from which it derives its knowledge, but, in its life and action, it is as independent of the senses as the painter is of the men who supply him with his brushes and colours. Since it can act without the aid of the body, it can exist even when the body perishes, and can continue to seek for truth and to love what is good.

(—*See Supplementary Notes, p.* 138.)

B.

## The Immortality of the Soul.

**The Soul is Immortal.**—(1) We have proved that the destruction of the body does not involve the destruction of the soul. The soul, unlike the body, is immaterial. It is not made up of parts distinct and separable. Therefore, after death, it cannot perish of itself or through the agency of any creature. God alone can destroy it.

(2) Since the desire of perfect happiness is common to all men, it must spring from human nature itself, and must have been implanted therein by God, whose wisdom and justice exclude the possibility of its universal frustration. Perfect happiness, therefore, is the Divinely appointed destiny of man, and must be attainable by all who act conformably to the Divine will. But perfect happiness in this world is beyond the reach of man. There must, therefore, be a future life in which it can be found.

(3) Conscience implies the existence of a Supreme Lawgiver who will reward the good and punish the wicked. It cannot be said that, in this life, the good and the wicked are uniformly treated according to their deserts. It happens only too often that the cunning malefactor succeeds in winning wealth and position, and that he ends his life untroubled by remorse and with a minimum of suffering, while the just man lives in toil and penury, and dies after a protracted agony, or freely sacrifices his life in the heroic discharge of duty. The justice of God, therefore, demands that there should be a future state in which this inequality is redressed.

(4) We are certain, then, that there is a life beyond the grave. But is it the Divine will that that life should endure for all eternity? Shall the good be granted but a limited period of happiness, undisturbed by the thought of approaching annihilation? No; their happiness must be of unlimited duration, as otherwise it would not be perfect happiness. And as for the wicked, when we consider the infinite majesty of God and His infinite claims to the obedience and gratitude of His creatures, their eternal punishment involves no incongruity. It must, however, be admitted that the proof from reason of the Immortality of the Soul presents many difficulties which cannot be satisfactorily solved without the aid of revelation.

## CHAPTER III.

NATURAL RELIGION. ITS INSUFFICIENCY. PROBABILITY OF REVELATION.

*Summary.*

I. Natural religion, defined. Its duties discoverable by the unaided reason. Man has duties :—
    A. Individually and socially, to God;
    B. To himself;
    C. To his neighbour.

II. A full and accurate knowledge of natural religion, practically unattainable without revelation :—
    (a) Man, unaided by revelation, has, as a fact, failed to acquire it;
    (b) Its discovery would be fruitless through defective teaching-authority.

III. The goodness and mercy of God lead us to the assurance that the necessary revelation has been made.

**I. Natural Religion. Individual and Social Duties.**—Natural religion is the sum of man's duties in so far as they can be ascertained by the light of reason alone.[1] From the truths already established, we infer that man has duties to God, to himself, and to his neighbour.

A. INDIVIDUALLY, MAN HAS DUTIES TO GOD.—(a) In God he recognises a Being of supreme excellence. (b) To God he owes his entire being and its preservation at every instant. (c) To God he owes all his faculties, or powers of acting: every throb of his heart, every glance of his eye, every thought of his mind, even the most trivial movements of soul or body are possible only with Divine aid or co-operation. (d) To God he owes his sense of right and wrong, and his sure hope that a good life will bring him great happiness. Man, therefore, perceiving his own inferiority and his total dependence on God, is bound to pay Him the supreme homage of adoration by acknowledging His supreme

---

[1] Supernatural Religion is the sum of man's duties as defined by Divine Revelation. Other definitions : Natural Religion is the worship of God prescribed by reason alone ; Supernatural Religion is the worship of God prescribed by Revelation.

excellence and by recognizing Him as his Creator, Preserver, and Sovereign Ruler. He is bound to thank Him and pray to Him as his Benefactor; to honour Him as the source of every perfection, to obey Him as his Master, and to feel and express sorrow for the offences he commits against Him.

SOCIALLY, MAN HAS DUTIES TO GOD.—(a) A society is a group of individuals united for a common purpose under a common authority.[2] The Family is a society for the rearing of children under the authority of their parents. The State is a number of families united under one government for the temporal well-being of all. (b) The Family is necessary for the very life of man, the State for his normal development. It is only in a well-ordered state that any degree of civilization is possible: its members are enabled to provide more conveniently, by division of labour, for the comforts and necessaries of life, and to promote by intercourse and mutual training the development of mind and heart. Since society, whether it consist of the Family or the State, is necessary for man, it follows that society is a Divine institution. It is a creature of God, indebted to Him for its existence and preservation, and for the benefits it receives; it can think and act through its governing authority; it, therefore, resembles a living person; it is conscious of its debt to God, and is under a like obligation to discharge it.[3]

Divine worship, naturally, in the case of individuals, necessarily, in the case of societies, must take some external, sensible form. Man, obeying the instincts God has given him, assumes a reverential posture at prayer, sets apart places for public worship, orders special ceremonies and rites, and appoints ministers to take charge of them.

B.—MAN HAS DUTIES TO HIMSELF.—God has given him his life and his faculties for use, not for abuse. He is, therefore, bound to take reasonable care of his life, to promote the health of mind and body, to be industrious, sober, and chaste.

C.—MAN HAS DUTIES TO HIS NEIGHBOUR.—Since social life is necessary to man, and since social life is impossible without truth-

---

[2] This definition is sufficient for our present purpose. A more exact definition is given in Chapter VIII. ("The Church.")

[3] Note that, even from the point of view of worldly advantage, the State should show individual citizens the good example of respect for religion. For, without the aid of religion, the State cannot secure permanently the two conditions on which its existence depends. Those conditions are (1) that the citizens deal justly with one another; (2) that they be loyal to the common authority.

fulness, justice, and obedience to lawful authority, it follows that these virtues and all others akin to them are prescribed by our nature, and, therefore, by God.

**II. A full and accurate knowledge of Natural Religion is practically beyond the reach of man.**—It must be borne in mind that, in arriving at the chief tenets of Natural Religion, we had the advantage of knowing them beforehand through revelation: we set about the solution of a question the answer to which we knew in advance.[4]

MAN, UNAIDED BY REVELATION, HAS, AS A FACT, FAILED TO ACQUIRE SUCH A KNOWLEDGE. But without the help of revelation it would be practically impossible to attain to a full and accurate knowledge of Natural Religion. Sufficient evidence for this is found in the failure of pagan nations and pagan sages. Among all the peoples of antiquity, the Jews alone excepted, the grossest errors prevailed. The Divine power in whose existence they believed was divided, they fancied, among two or more divinities. Their gods were at feud with one another; they were the patrons of theft, lying, and every disgraceful crime, and were offered a form of worship which in certain instances consisted of nothing less than public immorality. Men with such notions of the Deity had no fixed and unalterable standard of right and wrong. There was a universal belief in a future state, but the notion prevailed among cultured peoples, particularly the Greeks, that even for good men life after death was much less happy than life on earth, while less civilized races contemplated an endless career of low, sensual enjoyment. A study of the general character of religion and morality among the pagans of the present day leads us to similar conclusions.—Plato (428-347 B.C.), one of the masterminds of the world, favours in his ideal state a community of wives and the destruction of weakly and deformed children.[5] His great disciple, Aristotle (384-322 B.C.), who systematized so many branches of learning, held the same lax views as to the care of infant life; he allowed the exhibition in the temples of lewd figures of the gods; he had no proper conception of human dignity, and regarded the slave as a creature beneath the level of ordinary humanity, without a rational soul and with no more claim to consideration than the beast of burden.[6] It is true, however, that the moral code of the Roman Stoic philosophers, influenced possibly by the inspired books of the Jews, was remarkable for its elevation

---

[4] The chief duties of man according to the law of nature are expressed in the Ten Commandments (the third excepted).
[5] *Rep.* Book v.       [6] *Pol. iv. (vii.)* 16; 17, *I.* 5.

and purity, but still, Seneca, one of the leaders of the school, was emphatic in his approval of suicide, while Marcus Aurelius, its last and most perfect representative, hesitates, now approving, now condemning.

ITS DISCOVERY WOULD, IN ANY CASE, HAVE BEEN PROFITLESS FOR THE MASS OF MANKIND.—Through the promptings of nature itself, all men may know of the existence of God, or some Supreme Power, and their responsibility to Him. But the other truths and precepts of Natural Religion, the unity of God and the worship He should receive, the duties of man to himself and to his neighbour, all depend on reasoning so manifestly abstruse as to be within the reach of only the exceptional few, of rare talent and ample leisure. Let us make the supposition, which, as a fact, has never been realized, that in some community a gifted man of this description appears, that he masters all the truths of Natural Religion, that he devotes his life to the instruction of his fellows, and that he has no rival in ability to challenge his conclusions and impair his influence. Still his mission would fail for want of authority. A man tempted to sin would say: "This is forbidden by one liable to err like myself. All his reasoning may be false."

**The Probability of Revelation.**—Revelation, literally, "a drawing back of the veil," is a communication of truth made directly by God to man. We need not delay in proving that revelation is possible: God can communicate with men, for it was He who gave them the power to communicate with one another. The probability that He did give them a revelation is evident from what has been said of the unhappy condition of man in relation to his knowledge of Natural Religion and the Immortality of the Soul. The goodness and mercy of God lead us to the assurance that He would come to the rescue of the human race, that He would speak to them a word whose authority none could gainsay, that He would enlighten them as to their natural duties, and assure them of the immortality of the soul, and of judgment after death.

# CHAPTER IV.

## THE SIGNS OF REVELATION: MIRACLES AND PROPHECY.

*Summary.*

    The signs of Revelation: (a) nature of revealed doctrine; (b) miracles and prophecy.

    Miracles and prophecy, defined. Replies to the following objections against miracles :—

        A. That the evidence for miracles is necessarily unsatisfactory;

        B. That miracles are opposed to physical science;

        C. That alleged miracles need not be referred to Divine authorship.

    *Note.*—The proof of Revelation not dependent on a single miracle or prophecy.

**How Revelation may be known.**—We find certain men claiming that God has given them a revelation, and that He has commissioned them to speak in His name to the whole human race. We can know whether a teacher has been sent by God (1) if his doctrine be not unworthy of its alleged author; *e.g.*, it should not be ambiguous or trivial[7]; and (2) if it be confirmed by miracles or prophecies.

**Miracles and Prophecy, defined.**—A miracle is an occurrence outside the course of nature, perceptible to the senses, and explicable only as the direct act of God Himself. The possibility of miracles cannot be denied by anyone who admits the existence of a Personal God, the Creator of all things: He who fixed the course of nature can alter, suspend, or supersede it at His pleasure. A miracle is obviously a clear proof of the Divine origin of the doctrine in whose support it is wrought. The only

---

[7] We speak of conditions whose fulfilment can be recognized by ordinary men. Hence, we prefer to put the first condition as above, rather than say that the doctrine should be noble, elevating, agreeable to the reason, satisfying to human aspirations, and beneficial to society.

question to be decided in connection with miracles is whether, in a given case, a miracle has occurred or not. In other words the question of miracles is a question of evidence. Prophecy is the definite prediction of events which depend for their occurrence on the exercise of free will, whether it be the free will of God or of rational creatures, and which are of such a nature as to be beyond the possibility of guess or human prevision. God alone can know beforehand what a free agent will do and all the particular circumstances of his act. A prophecy, therefore, if fulfilled, is as conclusive of Divine authority as a miracle. The former can originate only in God's Omniscience, the latter only in His Omnipotence.

**Objections.**—A. The evidence for miracles is unsatisfactory.— 1. "It is contrary to all experience for miracles to be true, but it is not contrary to experience for testimony to be false. The balance of probability must always be against the miracle" (Hume's objection).—Reply:—(a) The objection says, in effect, that what usually does not happen can never happen. Therefore, we should refuse to believe in any new invention. We should have refused to believe in the aeroplane, *e.g.*, when we first heard of it, as contrary to all previous experience. (b) There is no conflict between universal experience and the testimony for any particular miracle There is, therefore, no question of weighing one against the other, and finding which is the more probable. The mass of mankind can testify, *e.g.*, that the dead cannot be brought back to life by any means that they have seen tried. This does not prove, however, that the dead cannot be brought back to life by means which they have not seen tried, *i.e.*, by the direct interference of God. Miracles are exceptional occurrences and of necessity outside the range of common experience.[8]

2. "The advance of physical science, and the deeper insight it has given us into the secrets of nature, has been fatal to credulity in every form, to belief in charms, magic, witchcraft, miracles, and astrology. Educated people now-a-days have no more faith in such things than in nursery fables. The Christian miracles belong to the childhood of the world, when men were prepared to believe almost anything." (The ordinary rationalist view.) Reply:— (a) Several eminent scientists of the present day believe firmly in spiritualism, which does not differ appreciably from magic or witch-

---

[8] This objection made some stir in its day, but has now been abandoned except by the unthinking.

craft. It is, therefore, incorrect to say that credulity, as the rationalists term it, is a thing of the past. (b) We admit that the great Christian miracles occurred in a very credulous age. Hence, we recognize that careful scrutiny of the testimony is necessary. We shall find that, in the case of the greatest and the all-important miracle of Christianity, viz., the Resurrection of Christ, the witnesses, no matter what may have been the character of their age, were not credulous, but were reluctantly prevailed on to believe.

B.—Miracles are opposed to physical science.—I. "Physical science claims that nature acts uniformly. The doctrine of miracles says it does not. Therefore, if we believe in miracles, we must reject physical science." Reply:—We do not differ with scientists as to the uniformity of nature. We hold with them the general law of nature that the same physical cause in the same circumstances will produce the same effect, but we maintain that, when God intervenes, the circumstances are no longer the same[9]: a new power has been introduced. His intervention is of rare occurrence and does not invalidate the work of the scientist whose conclusions are concerned only with normal cases.

2. "But an interference by God with the course of nature may involve a violation of the Law of the Conservation of Energy. If, e.g., the stones leave the quarry at the mere word of the miracle-worker and make themselves into a house, this must happen through the expenditure of some energy that did not previously exist." Reply:—(a) The Law of the Conservation of Energy, it is hardly necessary to say, has not been proved for the whole universe, but only for isolated systems.[10] If the total energy of an isolated system is observed to increase, the Law of Conservation requires nothing more than that the increase be ascribed to the entrance of some new energy. (b) The miracle referred to may have been due merely to a re-distribution of energy. According to physicists themselves, there are vast stores of energy in the universe on which the Creator could draw, if He did not wish to introduce new energy. (c) We need have no hesitation in admitting that a miracle is an effect produced independently of the laws of nature. With those laws alone the physicist is concerned, not with an agency extrinsic to them.

C.—Miracles need not be referred to Divine authorship.— 1. "Miracles may be the work of evil spirits." Reply:—Evil

---

[9] Man himself can interfere with the forces of nature. If he holds a stone in his hand, he is preventing the law of gravity from producing one of its effects.

[10] See Clerk Maxwell, *Matter and Motion*, p. 59. The Law is too loosely stated in some text books, as though it had been verified for the whole universe.

spirits can undoubtedly work apparent miracles, but evil spirits like all other creatures are dependent on God at every instant for their existence and power of acting. God will not permit them to involve us in inevitable deception. Their agency may be detected by the personal depravity of their human medium, or by the absurdity or wickedness of his doctrine.

2. "Miracles may be due to hypnotism." Reply:—Hypnotism, as a curative agency, is successful only in certain forms of nervous disease. As a general explanation of miracles it is obviously inadequate. See below, Ch. VII. (III.—A).

3. "We do not yet know all the forces of nature. So-called miracles may have been due to occult forces whose operation will some day be fully understood." Reply:—(a) We do not know everything that natural forces can do, but we certainly do know some things which they can never do.[11] We know, *e.g.*, that natural forces alone will never raise a dead man to life, or restore a missing limb.[12] (b) The objection assumes that miracle-workers had far more knowledge of natural forces than any modern scientist. To ascribe such knowledge to Christ, for instance, and the Apostles, who, from the human standpoint, were uneducated men, and who lived at a time when physical science was practically unknown, is to suppose a miracle as great as any. (c) The modern world has witnessed the utilization of natural forces previously unknown. Still, no natural forces can ever be utilized except specially constructed instruments or apparatus be employed. But workers of miracles used, in many instances, no means whatever, nothing but a word or a gesture.

**Note.**—It should be noted that the revelation which God gave men through Christ is supported, not by a single miracle or prophecy, but by many miracles and prophecies whose cumulative effect should compel conviction. It is supported by the Messianic prophecies, and by all the miracles of Christ during His life-time; by the miracle of His character and personality and by the crowning miracle of His Resurrection. It is sup-

---

[11] We do not know the lifting power of a man, but we do know that no man can lift a ton.

[12] The building up of tissue is a slow and detailed process, every stage of which is perfectly well known. A period of time, more or less protracted, is essential. The instantaneous cure of a wound or a fracture is beyond "the category of natural possibilities, unless the whole foundation of our medical knowledge is inaccurate," Windle, *The Church and Science*, p. 151.

ported by the miraculous spread of Christianity and the constancy of its martyrs. It is supported by the miraculous vitality of the Church which has survived innumerable dangers, and lives in undiminished vigour.

[Read *The Question of Miracles*, by Rev. G. H. Joyce, S.J.; Manresa Press, price 1s. 10d.]

We prove in the following chapters that the Christian religion was revealed to us by God; that it is the one and only true religion; that, therefore, all rival religions are false.

God might have revealed to man nothing more than the truths and precepts of natural religion. By believing those truths and by obeying those precepts, man would be entitled to very great happiness after death. Freed from all temptation and misery, he would derive an intense pleasure from the contemplation of God, as imaged in His creatures. But God Himself would be hidden from his eyes. God would seem to dwell in some separate world from which he was excluded. God would not be his friend and intimate.

In the revelation which God, as a fact, has given us, He has not only made certain for us the whole content of natural religion, but He has told us many truths which no human mind could have ever discovered, and He has appointed for us a destiny which no creature without His special aid could win. He has promised us the happiness of knowing Him intimately, of seeing Him as He is, of living with Him for ever, and of being filled by Him with every joy. No human tongue can tell the value of His gift to us, for the gift is God Himself. In the Christian revelation, therefore, the Bounty of God shines forth no less clearly than His Mercy: His Mercy has healed our wounds and restored us to health, while His Bounty has clothed us and enriched us; it has raised us, poor creatures of earth, from beggary to royalty; it has made us sons of the Most High, destined for unending happiness in the home of our Father.

# THE DIVINITY OF CHRIST.

## CHAPTER V.

### THE HISTORICAL VALUE OF THE GOSPELS, THE ACTS OF THE APOSTLES, AND THE EPISTLES OF ST. PAUL.

[*Note.*—In proving the Divinity of Christ we may follow one or other of two main lines of argument:—

1. We may argue (as below) from the New Testament writings considered as historical compositions; or,

2. We may argue from the Divine authority of the Church:—
(*a*) The Church is the work of God: proved by her marvellous growth, by her catholic unity—unity in faith, obedience, and worship, in spite of the vast numbers in her fold—by her stability in spite of the assaults of all the centuries, by her wondrous holiness, and fruitfulness in all good works. (*b*) The Church, therefore, is from God and speaks in His name. But, it is her central doctrine that Christ is God. Therefore, that doctrine is true.]

*Summary.*

The four Gospels, the Acts of the Apostles and the Epistles of St. Paul must be accepted as historical, if they satisfy the three tests of (*a*) genuineness; (*b*) integrity; and (*c*) veracity.

 *A.* The Gospels :

  (*a*) Their genuineness proved by external and internal evidence;

  (*b*) Their integrity assured, chiefly, by the reverence of the early Christians for the sacred text;

  (*c*) Their veracity established by the character and history of the writers, and by the impossibility of fraud.

 *B.* The Acts of the Apostles and the Epistles of St. Paul : genuineness, integrity, and veracity, similarly established.

 *C.* Views of adversaries.

**How we establish the Historical Value of the New Testament Writings.**—The four Gospels,[1] the Acts of the Apostles,[2] and the Epistles of St. Paul,[3] are the portions of the New Testament writings on which we chiefly rely to prove the Divinity of Christ, and the authority of the Church which He founded. As the Gospels are of special importance in our proof, we give at some length the arguments which show that, even though we abstract from all question of their inspiration and regard them as merely secular compilations, we must accept them as historical. A work must be accepted as historical, or, in other words, as a faithful narrative of past events, (a) if it be genuine, *i.e.* if it be the work of the author to whom it is ascribed; (b) if it be intact, *i.e.* if the text be substantially as it left the author's hand; (c) if its author himself be trustworthy, *i.e.*, if it be shown that he was well informed and truthful.

A.

THE HISTORICAL VALUE OF THE GOSPELS.

(a) **The Genuineness of the Gospels.**—The Gospels are the genuine work of the writers to whom they are ascribed:

I. *External evidence*—the testimony of Christian and non-Christian writers:—

1. Numerous texts from the Evangelists are quoted in the letters of Pope Clement (95 A.D.), St. Ignatius of Antioch (107

---

[1] Viz. of SS. Matthew, Mark, Luke, and John. The Gospels of SS. Matthew, Mark and Luke are called the Synoptic Gospels, because of their close resemblance in matter and arrangement: they give us, as it were, but one picture, not three distinct pictures, of Christ. St. Matthew wrote before St. Mark; St. Mark, between 50 and 60 A.D.; St. Luke, somewhat later. As Our Lord died about the year 30 A.D., these three Gospels were written within the lifetime of those who had seen and known Him. St. John's Gospel, written about 100 A.D., supplements the account of the other three; its distinctive feature is its report of the discourses of Christ, and the prominence which it gives to the arguments for His Divinity. The word "gospel" means "good tidings": the Gospels convey the good tidings of the coming of the Redeemer. The writers of the Gospels are called, from the Greek title, Evangelists.

[2] Written by St. Luke not long after he had completed his Gospel

[3] Written within the period 50-67 A.D.

A.D.), St. Polycarp of Smyrna (120 A.D.), and other disciples of the Apostles; also, in the *Shepherd* of Hermas (?150 A.D.), the Letter to Diognetus (?150 A.D.), and in the important work entitled *The Teaching of the Twelve* which was written, probably, as early as 95 A.D., but not later than 130 A.D.

2. (*a*) St. Justin[4] of Samaria and Rome, who became a Christian in 130 A.D., says that the Gospels were written by Apostles and disciples, and were read at the meetings of Christians on Sundays.

(*b*) Papias[5] of Phrygia, Asia Minor, disciple or associate of St. John, writing about 130 A.D., explains the circumstances in which the Gospel of St. Mark was composed, and refers to a work by St. Matthew, probably his Gospel.

(*c*) Tatian wrote his *Diatesseron*, or harmony of the four Gospels, about the year 170 A.D. Since the publication of the Arabic version in 1888, the genuineness of the work is no longer in dispute.

(*d*) St. Irenaeus,[6] writing about 180 A.D., says: "Matthew wrote a Gospel for the Jews in their own language, while Peter and Paul were preaching and establishing the Church at Rome. After their departure,[7] Mark, also, the disciple and interpreter of Peter, handed down to us in writing the information which Peter had given. And Luke, the follower of Paul, wrote out the Gospel which Paul used to preach. Later, John, the disciple of the Lord, who had reclined on His breast, published his Gospel during his sojourn at Ephesus in Asia Minor." The personal history of St. Irenaeus invests his testimony with special importance: a native of Asia Minor, in his early youth he drank in with avid ears, he tells us, the discourses of St. Polycarp who was himself a disciple of St. John, Apostle and Evangelist; he became bishop of Lyons in France, and lived for some time at Rome. His testimony, therefore, representing the tradition of East and West and of what was then undoubtedly the heart of Christendom, must be accepted as decisive.

(*e*) Tertullian of Africa, writing against the heretic Marcion, about 200 A.D., appeals to the authority of the churches, "all of which have had our Gospels since Apostolic times." He speaks of the Gospels as the work of the Apostles Matthew and John, and of the disciples Mark and Luke.

(*f*) Heretics, *e.g.* Basilides (†130 A.D.), and pagans, *e.g.* Celsus (†c. 200 A.D.), did not question the genuineness of the Gospels. Later

---

[4] Apol. I. 66, 67; Dial, cum Tryph., n. 103. [5] Quoted by Euseb. H.E. III., 39. [6] Adv. Haer. III., 1.
[7] The Greek is uncertain. The word may mean "death."

testimony is abndant. Probably there is not one of the pagan classics whose genuineness can be supported by such convincing evidence. No one disputes that Cæsar was the author of the Commentaries on the Gallic Wars, and yet the only ancient references to the work are found, about one hundred years after its composition, in the writings of Plutarch and Suetonius.

The fact that the Gospels were held in veneration and were in practical use all over the Church, within one hundred years of the death of the Apostles, and while their memory was still vivid, is a conclusive proof of their genuineness. Would the Apostles themselves or their immediate successors, who gave their lives to testify to the truth of all that is contained in the Gospels, have allowed a series of forgeries to be published, and palmed off as the inspired Word of God? Would Jewish converts have accepted them, without jealous scrutiny, as equal in authority to their own profoundly revered books of the Old Testament? Would the Gentiles, so many of them men of the highest education, have embraced a religion which made such severe demands on human nature, which exacted even the sacrifice of life itself in witness of the faith, without previously assuring themselves of the genuineness of its written sources? Would learned pagans and heretics have fastened on all kinds of arguments against the Church, and have neglected the strongest of all, viz. that its sacred books were forgeries? Would the faithful throughout the world, at a time when to be a Christian was to be a martyr, have all conspired without a single protest to fabricate and accept these books, falsely ascribe them to the Evangelists, and hand down the impious fraud as an everlasting inheritance for the veneration and guidance of their children's children? We must, therefore, either accept the Gospels as genuine, or commit ourselves to a series of puerile absurdities.

II. *Internal evidence*: an examination of the texts themselves proves that the writers were Jews; and were contemporaries, or in close touch with contemporaries, of the events they record :—

1. The writers were Jews : (a) The Gospels are written in Hellenistic Greek,[8] a form of the Greek language strongly marked by Hebrew idiom,[9] and employed as a literary medium by Jews during the first century of our era,[10] but not subsequently. (b) The writers show no acquaintance with Greek literature or philosophy, but are familiar with the religion, customs, and usages of the Jewish people.

2. The authors were contemporaries, or in close touch with contemporaries, of the events they narrate :— (a) Modern scholarship has failed to detect any error on the part of the Evangelists in their countless references to topography and to the political, social, and religious conditions of Palestine at the time of Christ. Those conditions, peculiarly complicated[11] and transient, could not have been accurately portrayed by a stranger to Palestine or by a late writer. The unsuccessful rebellion against the Romans (66-70 A.D.), which flung a devastating flood of war over the land, sweeping the Holy City and the Temple off the face of the earth, was followed

---

[8] The Gospel of St. Matthew was first written in Hebrew or Aramaic, and was shortly afterwards translated into Hellenistic Greek.

[9] e.g., the body is spoken of as "the flesh"; "soul" means life, temporal or eternal; "my soul" is sometimes used as the equivalent of the pronoun of the first person; abstract terms are avoided, e.g., "the meek," " the clean of heart," and other such expressions are employed instead of " meekness," " purity," etc.

[10] The writings of Philo Judaeus (?—50 A.D.), and some of the writings of Josephus, the Jewish historian, are in Hellenistic Greek.

[11] e.g., the government was administered in part by the Romans and in part by natives; the Sanhedrin, or great religious council of Jewish judges, still exercised its functions, and was in frequent conflict with the civil officials; taxes were paid in Greek money, Roman money was used in commerce, dues to the Temple were paid in Jewish money; the languages, Hebrew and Greek, and, to some extent, Latin, were spoken : in general, public and private life was affected in many ways by the diversity of language and the division of authority.

by enormous changes in population and government. A writer, therefore, who was not a contemporary of Christ, or in intimate relations with His contemporaries, would certainly have committed many errors when dealing with the period which preceded that great catastrophe. (b) The vividness of the narrative seems to spring from personal contact with the events recorded.

(b) **The Integrity of the Gospels.**—The Gospels have come down to us intact, *i.e.*, free from corruptions or interpolations. The purity of the text is assured by:—

1. The great reverence of the Church for the four Gospels and her rejection of all others.[12]

2. The practice which prevailed from the earliest times of reading the Gospels at public worship.[13]

3. The wide diffusion of the Gospels among Christian communities all over the world.

4. The substantial uniformity of the text in all manuscripts, some of which date from the fourth century.[14]

---

[12] Gospels ascribed to SS. Peter, Thomas and James were in circulation in the sub-apostolic age, but were suppressed by the Church as spurious.

[13] See above I. 2(*a*). The value of the guarantee of publicity may be measured from the incident recorded by St. Augustine (Ep. 71, 5; 82, 35) as having befallen one of his colleagues, an African bishop. He says that St. Jerome's use of the word "ivy" for "gourd," in his version of the prophecy of Jonas, caused such dissatisfaction when read out in church, that the bishop, fearing lest he might lose his people, felt compelled to restore the traditional rendering.

[14] A Syriac version dates from the second century. The oldest manuscript of Horace dates from the seventh or eighth century, of Cicero, Caesar, Plato from the ninth, of Thucydides and Herodotus from the tenth, of Aeschylus and Sophocles from the eleventh, of Euripides from the twelfth or thirteenth, yet no one doubts that these manuscripts are, substantially, the uncorrupted descendants of the originals. No one would ever have thought of questioning the integrity of the Gospel texts, but for the fact that they contain a Divine law of belief and conduct, irksome to the irreligious.

## THE DIVINITY OF CHRIST.

(c) **Trustworthiness of the Evangelists.**—The Evangelists are trustworthy, because they knew the facts and truthfully recorded them :—

1. They knew the facts: SS. Matthew and John had been companions of Christ; SS. Mark and Luke had lived in constant intercourse with His contemporaries.

2. They were truthful : (a) Their holy lives, and their sufferings in witnessing to the very truths set forth in their Gospels guarantee their sincerity. (b) From the world's standpoint, they had nothing to gain but everything to lose by testifying to the sanctity and the Divinity of Christ. (c) They could not, if they would, have been untruthful : they wrote for contemporaries of the events they narrate, or for men who had known those contemporaries, and could not, without detection, have published a false account. (d) Their narratives appear at some points to be irreconcilable, but can be harmonized by careful investigation. Had the Evangelists been impostors, they would have avoided even the appearance of contradiction. (e) They could not have invented their portrait of Christ. His character, so noble, so lovable, so tragic, so original, emerging unconsciously, as it were, with ever greater distinctness of outline, as the Gospel narrative proceeds, is, viewed merely as an artistic creation, quite beyond the inventive capacity of men such as the Evangelists were. Besides, every Jew of their day—and the Evangelists were Jews—believed that the Messias would come to restore the kingdom of David; not one of them ever dreamt, before the teaching of Christ, that He would come to found, not a temporal, but a spiritual kingdom, to preach meekness, humility, and brotherly love, and to live a life of poverty and persecution, culminating in the agony of the Cross.

## B.

## THE HISTORICAL VALUE OF THE ACTS OF THE APOSTLES AND THE EPISTLES OF ST. PAUL.

**The Acts of the Apostles.**—The opening words of the Acts and the Gospel of St. Luke prove identity of authorship. St. Irenaeus, who quotes several passages from the Acts, says that St. Luke was the companion of St. Paul and the historian of his labours. The Fragment of Muratori (second century) which contains the list of S. Scriptures says: " But the Acts of all the Apostles are in one book which, for the excellent Theophilus, Luke wrote, because he was an eye-witness of all." Similar statements are found in Tertullian, Clement of Alexandria, Origen and many others. Even the sceptic, Renan, declares: " a thing beyond all doubt is that the Acts have the same author as the third Gospel and are a continuation of the same." Harnack, a much greater authority, is of the same opinion. The arguments which prove the integrity of the text and the veracity of the author are similar to those advanced in the case of the Gospels, and need not be repeated.

**The Epistles of St. Paul.**—Our adversaries admit the genuineness of the epistles to the Romans, Corinthians, Galatians, Philippians, and Thessalonians; the other epistles, they say, with the exception of the Hebrews, were written under the direction or influence of the Apostle. We need not delay to establish the authority of the epistle which they reject or question, since it is not required for the purposes of our argument.[15]

## C.

**Views of Adversaries.**—(1) Strauss (1808-74) said that the Gospels were Christian myths, committed to writing about 200 A.D.; that they portray an ideal Christ; that of the real Christ we know nothing.—This view is not now regarded as within the domain of serious scholarship. It is mentioned chiefly to draw attention to the fact that, as the groundwork of some popular romances, it has sapped the faith of the ill-instructed.

(2) The latter-day representatives of the Tübingen school, founded by Baur (1792-1860), say that St. Paul is the real author of Christianity, the inventor of the Divinity of Christ, the Sacraments, and the doctrine of a visible Church. The Modernist school (Loisy and others) hold practically the same view.—Reply:

---

[15] See next paragraph 2.

(a) St. Paul suffered and died for the faith which he taught. He wrote at a time when very many who had listened to the teaching of Christ Himself were still living. Had he tried, he could not, undetected, have falsified the doctrine of his Master.

(b) We may add that " if Christ were not God, Paul could never have deified Him, and the Christians would never have admitted His Divinity, for the first Christians were Jews, and Jews were sensitive of blasphemy."[16]

(c) Harnack, a scholar of high repute among Rationalists, and the representative of the most recent phase of liberal criticism, says that the Synoptic Gospels were written before 70 A.D.[17]; that the Gospel of St. John, which he places between the years 80-118 A.D., does not possess the historical value of the Synoptics, but, still, that " it is one with them in their prevailing purpose to put prominently forward the divine sonship of Jesus."[18] Harnack, we observe, makes three most important admissions:—(1) that the dates we assign to the Gospels are substantially correct; (2) that the Synoptic Gospels are historical; (3) that they represent Christ as claiming to be the Son of God. The conclusions of Harnack are a triumph for the Church. The New Testament documents have been tried in the furnace of hostile criticism and have emerged unscathed.

[Read the section on the Gospels in *Jesus Christ is God*, by P. Courbet: C.T.S., price 7d.

---

[16] *The Synoptic Gospels in Recent Research*, Rev. P. Boylan, Maynooth Union Record, 1915-16.

[17] In the *Neue Untersuchungen zur Apostelgesch. und zur Abfassungsz, der Syn. Evang.*, 1911, Harnack places SS. Mark and Luke before 60.

[18] *Lukas der Arzt*, p. 118, Leipzig, 1906.

## CHAPTER VI.

### JESUS CHRIST CLAIMED TO BE GOD.

*Summary*

That Christ claimed to be God is proved:
  I. (1) From His words as reported in the Synoptic Gospels;
  (2) From His words as reported in the Gospel of St. John;
  II. From His acts.
  III. From the belief of His Apostles and disciples.

**I. (1) The Synoptic Gospels testify that Jesus claimed to be God.**—When Jesus stood before the Sanhedrin on Good Friday morning, " the High-priest asked Him and said to Him: Art thou the Christ the Son of the blessed God? And Jesus said to him: I am. And you shall see the Son of Man[1] sitting on the right hand of the power of God, and coming with the clouds of heaven. Then the High-priest rending his garments saith: What need we any further witnesses? You have heard the blasphemy. What think you? Who all condemned Him to be guilty of death."[2] The expression "son of God" is used sometimes in the Scriptures in the figurative meaning of "friend" or "servant of God." Had this been its sense here, the Sanhedrin would not have regarded it as blasphemous, that is, as insulting to God. Every Jew would be proud to call himself " son of God " in the loose meaning that he owed to God the gratitude and submission which a son owes to his father. The blasphemy consisted in the claim which Jesus was understood to make of true sonship, of oneness in nature with God. It was for that blasphemy they condemned Him to death.—One day, near Cæsarea, Jesus " asked His dis-

---

[1] Jesus speaks of Himself as "the Son of Man," a Messianic title see Bk. of Daniel, vii. 13, 14.
[2] St. Mark xiv. 61-64; cf. St. Matthew xxvi. 63-66.

ciples, saying: Whom do men say that the Son of Man is? But they said: Some John the Baptist, and other some Elias, and others Jeremias or one of the prophets. Jesus saith to them: But whom do you say that I am? Simon Peter answered and said: Thou art Christ, the Son of the living God. And Jesus answering said to him: Blessed art thou, Simon Bar-Jona, because flesh and blood hath not revealed it to thee, but My Father who is in heaven."[3] Here, again, there can be no question of figurative sonship. In this sense, John the Baptist, Elias and the prophets were " sons of God." Besides, had St. Peter used the words in this weaker meaning, he would not have required an inspiration from God, the Father.—Again He said to them: "All things are delivered to Me by my Father; and no one knoweth who the Son is but the Father; and who the Father is, but the Son."[4] Christ is, therefore, one in knowledge and authority with the Father.—He claims to sit in judgment on all mankind: " The Son of Man shall come in His Majesty, and all the angels with Him . . . and all the nations shall be gathered together before Him, and He shall separate them one from another."[5] It is only God who can speak of Himself thus. It is only God who can read the hearts of the countless millions of mankind, and apportion to each individual his deserts. In the continuation of the same passage, He will tell the good, He says, on the day of judgment that their acts of charity were not done to their fellow-men but to Him, and He will tell the wicked that the acts of charity which they failed to perform were denied not to their fellow-men but to Him. He identifies Himself, therefore, with God whom good men please and wicked men displease.—The Pharisees accused the disciples of Jesus of having violated the Sabbath. Jesus replied that " the Son of Man is

---

[3] St. Matt. xvi. 13-17.
[4] St. Luke x. 22; cf. St. Matt. xi. 25.
[5] St. Matt. xxv. 31, 32; cf. id. vii. 21-23

Lord even of the Sabbath."⁶ That is to say, the Sabbath observance may be set aside by Him, viz. God, who instituted it.—He said, in the Sermon on the Mount, " You have heard that it was said to them of old, thou shalt not kill . . . *But I say to you* that whosoever is angry with his brother, shall be in danger of the judgment."⁷ And, throughout the discourse, He returns repeatedly to the same emphatic declaration : " You have heard . . . *But I say to you.*" He represented Himself, therefore, as a Lawgiver, equal in authority to God Himself who gave the Commandments on Sinai. He claimed power to enlarge them and interpret them anew, because He claimed to be God, their Author.

(2) **The Gospel of St. John testifies that Jesus claimed to be God.**—Jesus said to the Jews : " I and the Father are one." They were about to stone Him for these words, " because," they said, " Thou being a man makest Thyself God."⁸—Jesus, replying to the Jews, who were offended because He had cured a sick man on the Sabbath day, said : " My Father worketh until now and I work." Whereupon "they sought the more to kill Him because . . . He said God was His Father, making Himself equal to God." Jesus, so far from saying that they had misunderstood Him, answered : " . . . what things soever [the Father] doth, these the Son also doth in like manner . . . For as the Father raiseth up the dead and giveth life so the Son also giveth life to whom He will."⁹—The Jews said to Him : " Thou art not yet fifty years old, and hast Thou seen Abraham? Jesus said to them : Amen, amen, I say to you, before Abraham was made, I am."¹⁰—" [The Father] hath given all judgment to the Son, that all men may honour the Son, as they honour the Father."¹¹—To Nicodemus He said : " He that doth not believe [in

---
⁶ St. Matt. xii. 8.  ⁷ *Id.* v. 21, 22 ; cf. 28, 32, 34, 39, 44.
⁸ St. John x. 30-33.  ⁹ *Id.* v. 17-21.  ¹⁰ *id.* viii. 57, 58.
¹¹ *id.* v. 22, 23.

the Son] is already judged : because he believeth not in the name of the only begotten Son of God."[12]—He speaks of Himself as "the door."[13] through which men enter into life; He is "the vine,"[14] we are the branches; He is "the Way, and the Truth, and the Life."[15]—Before He suffered, He prayed to His heavenly Father : "Glorify Thou Me, O Father with Thyself, with the glory which I had, before the world was, with Thee . . . And all My things are Thine, and Thine are Mine."[16] Many more texts of like purport from St. John and the other Evangelists might be quoted.[17]

II. **The Acts of Jesus testify that He claimed to be God.**—Jesus performed His many miracles, not merely as the ambassador of God, but as God Himself : "though you will not believe Me, believe the works," *i.e.* the miracles, "that you may know and believe that the Father is in Me, and I in the Father."[18]—He allowed men to adore Him as God. When He had given sight to the man born blind, He asked him : "Dost thou believe in the Son of God? He answered, and said : Who is He, Lord, that I may believe in Him? And Jesus said to him : . . . it is He that talketh with thee. And he said : I believe, Lord. And falling down, he adored Him."[19]—He forgave sin as of His own independent power. "Son, thy sins are forgiven thee," He said to the man sick of the palsy; and, when the Scribes ask themselves indignantly : "Who can forgive sins but God only?" He does not deny the assertion implied in their question, viz. "it is only God who can forgive sin," but goes on to re-affirm the claim He has already made : "that you may know that the Son of Man hath power on earth to forgive sins, (He saith to the sick of the palsy) Arise, take up thy bed

---

[12] *id.* iii. 18.    [13] *id.* x. 9.    [14] *id.* xv. 1.    [15] *id.* xiv. 6.
[16] *id.* xvii. 5, 10, 19.
[17] When Christ says, St. John xiv. 28, "the Father is greater than I," He means that "the Father is greater than I, *as man.*"
[18] *id.* x. 38.    [19] *id.* ix. 35-38 ; cf. St. Matt. xiv. 33 ; xv. 25 ; xvii. 14.

and go into thy house. And immediately he arose; and, taking up his bed, went his way in the sight of all."[20]— To Magdalen, who had kissed His feet and bathed them with her tears, He said : " Thy sins are forgiven thee." And to those who sat at table with Him on the same occasion, He said : " Many sins are forgiven her because she hath loved much." It is only through love of God that sins are forgiven. Christ, therefore, asserts that love of Him is love of God. In other words, He claims to be God.[21]

III. **The Apostles and Disciples believed that Christ was God.**—No one denies that, after the death of Christ, His followers, both Jews and Gentiles, preached His Divinity, and that they suffered and died in testimony thereof,[22] facts which can be explained only by their belief that He Himself had claimed to be the Son of God.

---

[20] St. Mark ii. 5-12.   [21] St. Luke vii. 48.
[22] Acts iii., 14, 15; v. 41; vii. 55-58; viii. 37; xv. 26; xx. 28

# CHAPTER VII.

## JESUS CHRIST, TRUE GOD.

We prove the Divinity of Christ by three arguments : [1]

   I. By His perfection as a man and as a teacher of natural religion, considered in the light of His claim to be God.
  II. By His Resurrection.
 III. *A.* By His miracles.
     *B.* By His prophecies.
     *C.* By the fact that He was Himself the fulfilment of prophecy.

## I.

### FIRST ARGUMENT.

**THE PERFECTION OF CHRIST AS A MAN AND AS A TEACHER OF NATURAL RELIGION, CONSIDERED IN THE LIGHT OF HIS CLAIM TO BE GOD, PROVES THAT HE WAS GOD.**

Outline of proof :—Christ, viewed from a merely human standpoint,[2] was the most perfect man, the most perfect teacher of Natural Religion that ever lived. Our adversaries proclaim it as well as we. But this most perfect man said repeatedly and emphatically that He was God. We must, therefore, conclude that His claim was just, that He *was* God ; otherwise, we are driven to the appalling absurdity of saying that the most perfect of mankind was either a maniac or a blasphemer.

**The Human Character of Christ.**—*His origin, His power over men, His eloquence, His silence* :—He came from Nazareth, a village in Galilee, the most backward district in Palestine. Men asked in wonder : " Can anything

---

[1] Arguments I. and II. are developed at some length. Argument III. is sketched in outline. Other arguments are given in the treatise on the Church.

[2] We disregard for the moment all direct evidence of His divinity.

good come from Nazareth?[3] . . . Is not this the carpenter, the Son of Mary?[4] . . . How doth this man know letters having never learned?"[5] Yet this poor tradesman had a power over the human heart which men could not resist. He called them and they came. They left their homes and their fathers, their boats, their nets, and their money and followed Him.[6]—He was gifted with a wondrous power of speech. He pressed a world of meaning into a short sentence. He employed the plainest and homeliest illustrations, *e.g.*, the woman searching for the lost piece of money, the patching of an old garment, the shepherd in quest of his sheep.[7] He clothed His thoughts in simple and beautiful language, as where He says of the lilies of the field that " not even Solomon in all his glory was arrayed as one of these."[8] By parables such as that of the Good Samaritan,[9] or the Prodigal Son,[10] he fixed His great doctrine of Love in the minds of the least instructed of His hearers. He touched at times a depth of pathos in such words as : "Come to Me, all you that labour and are burdened and I will refresh you ";[11] and, in His last discourse to His disciples, He speaks in the language of grave and tender sadness, full of the sorrow of parting and death, and yet breathing a sublime assurance that His work had not failed.[12] No wonder that men followed Him for days without food. Even His enemies said, " Never did man speak like this man."[13] He outmatched them in the gift of eloquence, and confounded them with His quick retort and subtle reply. Often they tried to ensnare Him into some awkward admission, but He baffled them by His wisdom.[14] And He could be silent as well as eloquent. At His trial, He answered when adjured to answer, but He was silent

---

[3] St. John vii. 41 ; i. 46.   [4] St. Mark vi. 2, 3.   [5] St. John vii. 15.
[6] St. Matt. iv. 18-22; ix. 9; St. Mark ii. 14.
[7] St. Matt v., vi., vii., x.   [8] *Id.* vi. 26-34.   [9] St. Luke x. 30-35.
[10] *Id.* xv. 11-32.   [11] St. Matt. xi. 28-30.   [12] St. John xiv.-xvii.
[13] *Id.* vii. 46.
[14] *e.g.* St. Matt. xii. 26-28 ; St. Luke xiii. 14-16.

while the witnesses were giving their perjured evidence. There was no need for speech, for they contradicted and confounded one another. Pilate, who knew that their testimony was worthless, still sought to provoke Him to reply, but " He answered him never a word, so that the governor wondered exceedingly."[15] And when Peter had denied Him, He spoke, not with His lips, but with His eyes. It was enough. " Peter going out wept bitterly."[16]

*He was a man of superb courage, and stainless character. He was firm but not obstinate.*—The poor tradesman from Galilee had no fear of the proud and powerful Pharisees. He scourged them in a terrible invective for their hypocrisy, their avarice, and their hardness of heart. He knew that their fury could be sated only by His blood, yet He never ceased to whip them with the lash of righteous indignation.[17] Several times He was on the brink of destruction. Once a raging mob had swept Him to the verge of a cliff, but, at the last moment, He eluded their grasp.[18] In the hour of His Passion, caught in the toils of His enemies, He made no appeal, no apology, no retractation of His doctrine. No cry for mercy escaped Him, when the pitiless scourges lacerated His flesh, nor when His sacred hands and feet were nailed to the Cross.—Bitter though His enemies were, they were silent when He challenged them to charge Him with sin:[19] He was the only man that ever lived who could stand up before His enemies and defy them to convict Him of a single fault. The traitor, Judas, confessed, " I have sinned in betraying innocent blood."[20] At His trial, when His foes strained every nerve against Him, neither

---

[15] St. Luke xxiii. 14; St. Matt. xxvii. 13, 14.
[16] St. Luke xxii. 61, 62.
[17] St. Matt. xxiii.; xvi. 21; St. John xi. 48.
[18] St. Luke iv. 30; cf. St. Matt. xii. 15; St. John viii. 59; x. 39; xi. 53.
[19] St. John viii. 46.    [20] St. Matt. xxvii 14.

Pilate nor Herod could find any guilt in Him[21]: His character scrutinized in the fierce light of savage hatred showed not a stain.—He was no self-seeker, no respecter of wealth. He fled when the multitude sought to make Him king.[22] He had not enough money to live without alms.[23] He could not pay the temple dues without a miracle.[24] He whose ability might have borne Him to the highest position had not " whereon to lay His head ";[25] He preferred to be a teacher of truth, to wander about poor and homeless.—He was firm, but not obstinate. He refused to abate His teaching to win the companionship of the wealthy young ruler.[26] Yet, He knew how to bend when no principle was at stake. He sought to escape, even by hiding, the importunities of the Syro-Phœnician woman who implored Him with piteous cries to heal her daughter, but, at last, touched by her profound humility, He yielded.[27]

*He was affable, gentle, courteous, and humble. He was a man of loving heart:*—He did not shun the companionship of men, His enemies murmured because He ate " with publicans and sinners."[28] Though Jews were not wont to converse with Samaritans, He spoke to the Samaritan woman at the well.[29] He was entertained at the house of his friends, Martha, Mary, and Lazarus.[29]—He gently remonstrated with His two Apostles, James and John, for their ambition.[31] He was courteous to the Pharisee, Nicodemus, because he came to Him with a right intention.[32] He impressed more than once on His Apostles the need of humility. They were not to lord it over their dependants like earthly princes. They were to be the servants of their subjects. He Himself set them the

---

21 St. Luke xxiii., 13-15.
22 St. John vi. 15.    23 St. Luke viii. 3.    24 St. Matt. xvii. 23-26.
25 *Id.* viii. 19, 20.
26 St. Mark x. 22.    27 St. Matt. xv. 24; St. Mark vii. 24.
28 St. Matt. ix. 11; St. Luke xv. 2; xix. 7.    29 St. John iv.
30 *Id.* xi. 5.    31 St. Matt. xx. 20.    32 St. John iii. 1-21.

example by washing their feet at the Last Supper.[33] He was a Man of loving heart. His three years' ministry was an incessant outpouring of love. The sick and the sinful came in vast numbers to Him. He healed them of their infirmities. His life was a daily triumph over sin, sorrow, and disease :—He saved from death the unhappy woman, convicted of a shameful crime : " He that is without sin among you," He said to her accusers, " let him first cast a stone at her,"[34] and looking into their consciences they slunk away ashamed; He restored the widowed mother her only son as he was being carried forth for burial; He feared not to lay His hands on the foul leper.[35] He wept with passionate grief over the Sacred City, dear to Him and to all Jews as the very hearthstone of their race : " How often would I have gathered thy children, as the hen doth gather her chickens under her wings, and thou wouldst not."[36] Some great light of love must have shone in His face, else why were little children brought to Him that He might notice them? He chid the Apostles for trying to keep them back. He took them in His arms and blessed them.[37] On the Cross, His heart was still the same loving heart, true to its old affections, ready to receive the sinner and to pardon the persecutor and calumniator. Amid all His agony, He thought of His Blessed Mother, and asked St. John to be a son to her; with words of sublime hope, He blessed the contrition of the penitent thief who, but a moment before, had been reviling Him; He besought His heavenly Father to pardon the very men who had nailed Him to the Cross, and who, even as He prayed for them, still pursued Him with mockery, insult, and blasphemy.

*Summary* : *He was the model of all virtues.*— To a perfect love for God and submission to His holy

---

[33] *Id.* xiii.    [34] *Id.* viii. 1-10.    [35] St. Mark i. 41.
[36] St. Matt. xxiii. 37. Cf. St. Luke xix. 42-44.
[37] St. Mark x. 14-16. See also, *Id.* ix. 35.

will ("Not My will but Thine be done"),[38] He united in a form, never before witnessed by men, the virtues of humility, patience, meekness, and charity. He was a brave, strong man, who spoke His mind fearlessly, and died for the doctrine He advocated. He was gentle, courteous, affable, and unselfish. No contradiction, calumny, or persecution could wring from Him a word or gesture inconsistent with His dignity as a heaven-sent instructor of mankind. His goodness was without weakness; His zeal and earnestness, without impatience; His firmness, without obstinacy. He was not only a thinker, but a man of action. His eyes seemed ever fixed on heaven, but yet He was full of sympathy for the weakness of His disciples, full of tenderness for the sorrowful and the afflicted, and He combined an intense hatred of sin with an intense love for the sinner. He is the model for men of all conditions in all ages, the ideal which, while remaining unattained and unattainable, has been the inspiration of the noblest lives.

THE TESTIMONY OF RATIONALISTS.—All who have studied the Gospels, unbelievers as well as believers, are agreed as to the nobility of the human character of Christ. Lecky, a Rationalist, says: "It was reserved for Christianity to present to the world an ideal character, which through all the changes of eighteen centuries has inspired the hearts of men with an impassioned love; has shown itself capable of acting on all ages, nations, temperaments, and conditions; has been not only the highest pattern of virtue, but the strongest incentive to its practice, and has exercised so deep an influence that it may be truly said that the simple record of three short years of active life has done more to regenerate and soften mankind, than all the disquisitions of philosophers, and all the exhortations of moralists."[39]

---

[38] St. Luke xxii. 42.
[39] History of European Morals, Vol. II., p. 8. 3rd ed. : Longmans, Green, and Co., London, 1911.

**Christ as a Teacher of Natural Religion.**—Christ, perfect as a man, was perfect as a teacher of Natural Religion. He stands alone and unrivalled because of His doctrine of the Law of Charity, His doctrine of the Law of Sincerity, His doctrine of the supreme importance of the human soul, and His ideals of moral perfection. He taught as "one having power," not like Socrates and others, as though He were groping for the light. He taught with clearness and decisiveness, and was Himself the model of all His teaching.

*His doctrine of the Law of Charity* :—The Jews of His day held high dispute as to which was the greatest commandment of their Law. Some said it was the commandment to offer sacrifice; others, the commandment of Sabbath observance; others, again, the commandment of Circumcision. Christ swept aside all current opinion as so much rubbish, and laid bare the true foundation of sanctity. "The whole Law," He said, in effect, "is summed up in the one Law of Charity, *i.e.* the love of God and one's neighbour."[40] But, in His Sermon on the Mount, the first great exposition of His teaching, He gave the Law of Charity a wider interpretation. "Neighbour," with the Jews, had meant a fellow Israelite or a friendly alien. Christ broadened its meaning so as to include every man without exception, good or wicked, friend or foe. Men must love one another, because they are brothers. They are brothers, because they are children of the same heavenly Father who loves them all, who gives the blessings of His Providence, the sunshine and the fruitful rain, to all, unjust as well as just, who goes in quest of the sinner, as the shepherd seeks for his lost sheep, who is no longer robed in the lightnings of Sinai, but shines with the radiance of kindness and love. Men must forgive one another as they hope to be forgiven. For how

---

[40] Cf. St. Matt. xxii. 37-40.

can they ask of their Father what they themselves refuse to a brother? Christ's Law of Charity, therefore, may be briefly expressed thus: "Love God, for He is your loving Father. Love and be indulgent to one another, for you are all His children. Love and forgive, as you hope to be loved and to be forgiven." Christ, unlike all other teachers, drew men close to God. He taught them to turn to God with a warm, personal love, and to see His image in their fellow-man.[41]

*His doctrine of the Law of Sincerity*:—Christ would have no mere outward sanctity, the sanctity of the Scribes and Pharisees who made light of internal sin. "Ye fools," He said to them, "did not He that made that which is without, make also that which is within?"[42] God is as much the author of the inner as the outer man, and will have service of them both. We must pluck anger and all uncleanness from our hearts. Our sanctity must be sound to the core.[43]

*His doctrine of the supreme importance of the human soul*:—The human soul is infinitely more precious than anything else in the world. The loss of friends, the loss of all our possessions, the loss of life itself are all as nothing compared with the loss of the soul: "What doth it profit a man, if he gain the whole world, and suffer the loss of his soul? Or what shall a man give in exchange for his soul? Whosoever shall save his life shall lose it, and whosoever shall lose his life for My sake and the gospel shall save it."[44] Others before Christ had perceived this truth, but dimly and as through a veil. He was the first to give it clear and fearless expression.

*His ideals of moral perfection*:—Poverty, virginity, and the complete abnegation of self were His ideals of moral perfection: "Sell all thou hast and give to the

---

[41] St. Matt. v., vi., vii.
[42] St. Luke xi. 40.
[43] St. Matt. v. 23-30.
[44] St. Mark viii. 35, 36.

poor ";[45] " if any man will come after Me, let him deny himself, and take up his cross daily and follow Me."[46] " Blessed are they that mourn . . . blessed are they that suffer persecution for justice sake."[47]

**Note**—1. (*a*) Had Christ not been God, or one sent by God, His teaching on natural religion would have failed for want of authority. (*b*) Clear though His teaching was in its main purport, it is obscure in some points. For instance, we are not always sure whether the heroic virtues which He commends are for all, or only for the few, or how in individual cases His doctrine should be applied. Hence the necessity of having always with us a living, infallible voice authorized to speak in His name, and to give the true interpretation.

2. Socrates (469-399 B.C.) is regarded as the noblest man of pagan antiquity, but he cannot be compared with Our Saviour. Socrates was the foe of pretended knowledge. He urged men to strive after precise ideas of goodness, holiness, justice, beauty, etc. He was put to death by the Athenian democracy in a moment of frenzy, not because of his supposed doctrines or method, but because of the profligacy and disloyalty of some of his companions. Though superior to his contemporaries in intellectual power, he shared the loose notions of his day in regard to chastity. He concerned himself only with the better educated among the Athenians. Even these he did not so much instruct as stimulate to inquiry. He undoubtedly helped to purify the gross popular notion of the Deity, but his ideas about a future state were vague in the extreme, and he had no conception of the brotherhood of man. Since he was born into a highly cultured state, and had as his contemporaries men of the first rank in philosophy, history, and art (*e.g.*, Anaxagoras, Thucydides, Euripides), the development of his talent was, in great measure, due to environment. Our Saviour, if we view Him from the human standpoint, enjoyed no such advantage. He spent His youth and manhood among peasants or artisans of little or no education.

THE TESTIMONY OF RATIONALISTS.—The German philosopher, Kant, says : " We may readily admit that, had not the Gospels first taught the general moral principles (*i.e.* the precepts of natural religion) in their full purity, our intellect would not even now understand them

---

[45] St. Luke xviii. 22.  [46] *Id.* ix. 23.  [47] St. Matt. v. 5, 10.

so perfectly." Harnack,[48] who does not admit that there was anything supernatural in Christ, cannot find words sufficiently emphatic to express admiration for His moral teaching. His sayings and parables, he says, are simplicity itself in their main purport, and yet they contain a depth of meaning which we can never fathom; in His personality, He is not like an heroic penitent or an enthusiastic prophet who is dead to the world, but He is a man who has rest and peace in His own soul and who can give life to the souls of others; He speaks to men as a mother speaks to her child. It is unnecessary to quote the opinions of other rationalists. All are agreed that Christ in His character and His doctrine was immeasurably beyond the noblest teachers that ever lived.

**Conclusion.**—It is admitted, therefore, that Christ was perfect as a man, was unsurpassed, unequalled as a teacher. But Christ claimed emphatically and persistently that He was God. We must admit that His claim was just, that He *was* God, or else face the terrible conclusion that He was a deceiver or a victim to some hallucination; in other words, we must say that the most perfect of mankind was a shameless liar and blasphemer or a pitiable maniac. Such is the colossal absurdity to which Rationalists are reduced, an absurdity which, when they realize it, must convince them that their entire position is untenable.[49]

---

[48] *What is Christianity?* II. (end); Engl. Trans.

[49] In arguing with Rationalists, we regard Christ merely as a teacher of natural religion, that is, as a teacher of moral truths which, in their entirety, it is not impossible for the unaided intellect of man to discover. We must not forget that Christ taught another and an incomparably higher doctrine, a doctrine which the human mind, unillumined by Divine grace, could never have conceived, and that from this fact we may argue, with even greater force, that He could not have been mere man.

## II.

### SECOND ARGUMENT.

### THE RESURRECTION OF JESUS CHRIST PROVES THAT HE WAS GOD.

Outline of Proof :—Christ claimed to be God; Christ said He would rise from the dead; Christ rose from the dead; therefore, Christ is God. The witnesses to the Resurrection were trustworthy. Refutation of adversaries' Theories : the Deception Hypothesis; the Hallucination Hypothesis; the Trance Hypothesis.

**Christ said He would rise from the dead.**—When the Jews demanded a miracle in proof of His authority, He answered : "Destroy this temple and in three days I will raise it up."[50] "He spoke," the Evangelist says, "of the temple of His body." Later He speaks more clearly : "An evil and adulterous generation seeketh a sign; and a sign shall not be given it, but the sign of Jonas the Prophet. For as Jonas was in the whale's belly three days and three nights, so shall the Son of Man be in the heart of the earth three days and three nights."[51] After the Transfiguration He says to Peter, James, and John : "Tell the vision to no man, till the Son of Man be risen from the dead."[52] Before going up to Jerusalem to suffer, He says with perfect distinctness : "Behold we go up to Jerusalem, and the Son of Man shall be betrayed to the chief priests and the scribes, and they shall condemn Him to death, and shall deliver Him to the Gentiles to be mocked and scourged and crucified, and the third day He shall rise again."[53] That He had foretold His Resurrection was well known to all, for the Jews, after His death, said to Pilate : "We have remembered that that seducer said, while He was yet alive, After three days I will rise again."[54]

---

[50] St. John ii., 19.  [51] St. Matt. xii. 39, 40  [52] Id. xvii. 9.
[53] Id. xx. 18, 19.  [54] Id. xxvii. 63.

**Christ died and was buried.**—The four Evangelists say that He died on the cross. The soldiers, finding Him already dead, did not break His limbs. One of them opened His side with a spear. When Joseph of Arimathaea asked Pilate for permission to bury Him, Pilate, before consenting, despatched a centurion to make sure that He was dead.[55] It was not likely that His enemies would leave their work half finished. In the words quoted above (end of last paragraph) they say "while He was yet alive," *i.e.* they assert that He is now dead.[56]

**Christ rose from the dead.**—The Evangelists tell us that the grave was found empty on the morning of the third day; that Christ appeared to Mary Magdalen and the other women; that He appeared to the Apostles and showed them His wounds, "See My hands and feet that it is I myself. Handle and see, for a spirit hath not flesh and bones as you see me to have"[57]; that He conversed with them and ate with them[58]; that He walked with the two disciples to Emmaus, and was recognised by them "in the breaking of bread."[59] "He was seen," St. Paul writes to the Corinthians, "by more than five hundred brethren at once . . . last of all He was seen by me."[60] The witnesses of the Resurrection are trustworthy :—(1) They were not deceivers. They had no inducement to give false testimony. Their labours, their sufferings, the very success of their preaching, are proofs of their sincerity. (2) They were not themselves deceived. If they were, they must have been deceived either (*a*) by their own imagination, or (*b*) by Christ Himself. They were not deceived by their

---

[55] St. Mark xv. 43-45.
[56] The Roman historian Tacitus (55-120 A.D. approx.) says that "Christus was put to death by the procurator, Pontius Pilate, in the reign of Tiberius," Annals xv. 44.
[57] St. Luke xxiv. 39.     [58] *id.* xxiv. 43.     [59] *id.* xxiv. 35.
[60] i. Cor. xv. 6, 8.

own imagination: the supposition is excluded by their numbers, their great incredulity, and the length of time that Christ was with them after His death. They were not deceived by Christ Himself: if they were, then we must suppose against the most explicit evidence that He did not die on the cross, but merely swooned, that He, the noblest and holiest of men, pretended to rise from the dead in order to send His disciples into the world to preach a lie, and that God blessed with miraculous success a work founded on fraud and blasphemy. The foregoing argument is more fully developed in the following paragraphs.

**Adversaries' Theories.**—*Deception Hypothesis.*—This was the earliest attempt to explain away the Resurrection and is an attack on the sincerity of the disciples. The guards at the sepulchre said that they fell asleep, and that, while they slept, the disciples came and removed the body[61]. The story spread widely among the Jews and many believed it. If the soldiers fell asleep, they could not have known what happened during their sleep; all they could have said was that, when they woke, the grave was empty. They might have added that *probably* the disciples came and stole away the body. Let us assume that they put their statement in some such reasonable form. Can we imagine that the disciples, who had shown utter timidity during the Passion, would risk liberty, perhaps life, in an attempt to steal the body, and all with a view to fraud? And why perpetrate such a fraud? If they really knew that Christ was not risen, then they knew He had deceived them and was not God. What had they to gain by preaching a fraudulent resurrection? Nothing but persecution, incessant labour, and death, not to speak of remorse of conscience. On the other hand, had they gone to the chief priests and denounced Christ as an impostor, they would have been amply rewarded. But, in spite of all worldly inducements to close their lips about the risen Christ, in spite of the opposition and hatred they knew awaited them, should they venture on even an indirect presentment of such a doctrine, they came boldly before the people on Pentecost Day, and put the Resurrection in the forefront of their preaching. On

---

[61] St. Matt. xxviii. 13. The Evangelist says they were bribed to make this statement.

that day, in Jerusalem itself, three thousand Jews[62] were converted by St. Peter to belief in Christ, Whom, he said, " God hath raised again, whereof all we are witnesses . . . neither did His flesh see corruption."[63] Some days later St. Peter spoke of Him as " the author of life . . . whom God hath raised from the dead."[64] Converts of every rank and race multiplied rapidly,[65] and within a few years might be counted by millions. Like their teachers, they had nothing to gain by their faith but tribulation and death. They must, therefore, have been absolutely convinced of the sincerity of the Apostles. St. Augustine says that, had not the Resurrection been a fact, the conversion of the world by a few Galilean fishermen to belief in it would have been as great a miracle as the Resurrection itself.

*The Trance Hypothesis.*—This suggests that Christ did not really die on the cross; He merely swooned; He recovered consciousness in the sepulchre; He pushed aside the stone and rejoined His companions; and so He made on them the impression that He had triumphed over death.—The mental anguish which Christ had suffered, the scourging, the crowning with thorns, the crucifixion, the piercing of His side with a spear make the trance hypothesis impossible. Suppose for a moment it were true, could one so severely wounded, so exhausted from loss of blood, have moved aside the great stone?[66] Could he have played the rôle of victor over death, and walked like one in perfect health with those cruel wounds in His feet? Could He have entered the supper-room through closed doors? Could He have appeared and disappeared at will? Could He make a vast concourse of disciples fancy that He ascended into heaven in their sight? Are we to suppose that this Man of perfect holiness, Who had suffered the agony of the Cross in upholding His claim that He was the Son of God, was a vile impostor; that He could set His followers on fire with zeal to go

---

[62] The Resurrection had taken place but a few weeks before. Each of these converts, therefore, could examine the witnesses for himself. And there were very many witnesses, for St. Paul tells us that "He was seen by Cephas (St. Peter), and after that by the eleven; then was He seen by more than five hundred brethren at once," i. Cor. xv., 5, 6.

[63] Acts ii. 32, 31.

[64] Acts iii. 15; cf. iv. 10. Five thousand were converted on this day: Acts iv. 4.—St. Paul says: " If Christ be not risen again, then is our preaching vain, and your faith is also vain," i. Cor. xv. 14.

[65] " A great multitude also of the priests obeyed the faith," Acts vi. 7.

[66] The women wondered whether they could find anyone to roll back the stone from the mouth of the sepulchre, "for it was very great," St. Mark xvi. 4.

forth and preach a lie to the world? Even the Rationalist Strauss rejects the hypothesis as unworthy of consideration.

*The Hallucination Hypothesis.*—This is the favourite hypothesis of modern adversaries. The followers of Christ, they say, were in a state of tense nervous excitement after the Crucifixion; they believed that their beloved Master would triumph over the grave and come back to them again; it was in answer to their passionate longing for His coming that their fancy bodied forth the vision of the risen Saviour.—That an individual might suffer from such an hallucination is possible; that all the Apostles and hundreds of the disciples should suffer from it simultaneously and over a long period is impossible. Besides, the evidence against the existence of any " passionate longing " is overwhelming. The followers of Christ were not expecting His Resurrection. When He was seized by the Jews, they fled in terror, believing that all was over. He had undoubtedly foretold His Death and Resurrection, but they appear never to have reconciled themselves to the thought of His Death and so did not think of His Resurrection.[67] Mary Magdalen and the other women brought spices to embalm His body on the morning of the third day. They, therefore, did not expect to find Him risen from the dead. Magdalen's first thought, when she saw the empty tomb, was that someone had stolen the Body.[68] When Christ spoke to her, she did not recognize Him at first, believing that He was the gardener. Cleophas and the other disciple, as they talked sadly of Christ on the road to Emmaus, told the stranger, as they thought Him, how they had been frightened by the women's story of the Resurrection. When He revealed Himself to them as Christ, they returned and told the Apostles. The Apostles refused to believe them, just as they had already refused to believe the women.[69] St. Thomas was not present when Christ first appeared to the Apostles, and protested that he would not believe, until he had put his finger " into the place of the nails " and his hand " into His side."[70] The witnesses, therefore, to the risen Christ were not credulous, but incredulous, and the hypothesis of hallucination is excluded.

**Conclusion.**—We have proved, therefore, through the testimony of friends and enemies that Christ died and was buried; we have proved through the testimony of witnesses who were honest and, at the same time, incredulous, and through the success which attended the

---

[67] St. Matt. xvi. 21, 22; St. Luke xxiv. 13-27, 44-46; St. John xx. 9.
[68] St. John xx. 13.   [69] St. Mark xvi. 11, 13.   [70] St. John xx. 25.

preaching of the Apostles, that Christ rose from the dead. Christ claimed to be God. Christ said He would rise from the dead. He rose from the dead. Therefore, Christ is God.[71]

*Celsus's Objection.*—Why did not Christ show Himself publicly after His Resurrection to His enemies and the entire people? That question was first asked by the pagan, Celsus (†c. 200 A.D.), and has been repeated by Renan and others.—(1) God wishes us to turn to Him freely, and, as a rule, does not employ a superabundance of means to bend the will of the evil-minded. He is content with giving clear, and amply sufficient proofs, that faith is reasonable. The rich man in the parable,[72] calling out from hell to Abraham, besought him to send a messenger from the dead to warn his five brothers of the tortures of the damned. Abraham refused, saying: "'They have Moses and the prophets. Let them hear *them*.' If they hear them not, ' neither will they believe if one rise again from the dead.'" The Pharisees asked Christ for a sign from heaven and were refused.[73] While He hung on the Cross, they that passed by bade Him come down, if He were the Son of God,[74] but he paid no heed to them. To one adversary He gave an exceptional grace: He appeared to the persecutor, Saul of Tarsus, afterwards the Apostle Paul.[75] (2) Had Christ appeared to all, the depraved subtlety of men would still have found a means to escape belief. "This is not Christ," they would have said, "but some evil spirit, an emissary of Satan." And unbelievers of later generations would probably ask: "If Christ appeared to all men after His Resurrection, why does He not appear to all men now? Why does He not remain on earth always?" Even though He did remain on earth always, these same unbelievers would still persevere in their incredulity, protesting that He was being personated by a series of impostors.

---

[71] No one who admits the Resurrection of Christ can deny the existence of God. If Christ rose from the dead, there must be a God who raised Him to life. The existence of God, therefore, is established by the Resurrection quite independently of the philosophical proofs at the beginning of the treatise.

[72] The parable of Lazarus and the rich man : St. Luke xvi. 19-31.
[73] St. Mark viii. 11-13.   [74] St. Matt. xxvii. 40.   [75] Acts ix.

## III.

### OTHER PROOFS OF THE DIVINITY OF CHRIST.

*A. His Miracles prove His Divinity.*—Besides the Resurrection, Christ performed many other miracles. He healed the sick, the blind, the lame, the dumb, the epileptic by a mere word, and sometimes from a distance; specially remarkable was the cure of the man born blind.[76] He raised the dead to life: the daughter of Jairus, the widow's son of Naim, and Lazarus. He delivered men from evil spirits, thereby showing His dominion over the world of spirits. Many of His miracles were wrought on inanimate nature: He changed water into wine; He fed five thousand with five loaves and two fishes; He stilled a storm with a word; He walked upon the waters. His miracles cannot be explained away: —(a) by *the delusion theory* according to which merely natural occurrences were regarded as supernatural by His credulous disciples, because the miracles were performed in public and their genuineness was not disputed by Christ's adversaries.[77] Nor (b) by *the theory of diabolical agency*, because Christ was holy in His person and in His doctrine, and could not, therefore, have been an emissary of Satan; Christ, by casting out evil spirits, showed that He was not the agent of Satan, but his enemy. Nor (c) by *the theory of hypnotism, or animal magnetism*. Certain nervous disorders may be cured by hypnotism or suggestion, but the cure cannot be effected instantaneously, nor from a distance; Christ cured all manners of diseases; in many cases the patients were not present and did not even know that He was about to cure them; the theory takes no account of cases of resurrection from the dead.

Christ appealed to His miracles as a proof that He was sent by God: "the works themselves which I do give testimony of Me that the Father hath sent Me."[78] Christ's teaching, therefore, was the teaching of God. But Christ taught that He Himself was God. Therefore, Christ is God.

*B. His Prophecies prove His Divinity.*—Christ foretold many things which came to pass and which no mere man could have foreseen:—(1) With reference to Himself, He foretold His Passion, Resurrection, and Ascension into Heaven;[79] (2) with reference to His disciples, He foretold that Judas would betray Him, that Peter would deny Him, that all His disciples would forsake Him;[80] (3)

---

[76] St. John ix.  [77] *id.* xi. 47.
[78] *id.* v. 36.  Cf. *id.* x. 37.  St. Matt. xi. 4, 5.
[79] St. John iii. 14; St. Matt. xx. 18; St. John vi. 63.
[80] St. John xiii. 21, 26; St. Matt. xxvi. 34; *id., ibid.*, 31

with reference to His Church, He foretold that it would grow like the mustard-seed, that it would leaven all mankind, that the gates of hell would not prevail against it.[81] The fulfilment of these prophecies proves that Christ's teaching was the teaching of God. But Christ taught that He was God. Therefore, Christ is God.

His prophecy about Jerusalem and the Jews is particularly noteworthy. He said: "The days shall come upon thee, and thy enemies shall cast a trench about thee, and compass thee round, and straiten thee on every side, and beat thee flat to the ground, and thy children who are in thee, and they shall not leave in thee a stone upon a stone."[82] And again: "There shall be great distress in the land, and wrath upon this people, and they shall fall by the edge of the sword, and shall be led away captives into all nations, and Jerusalem shall be trodden down by the Gentiles."[83] How accurately these prophecies were fulfilled will be understood by readers of the "History of the Jewish War," written, in seven books, by Flavius Josephus[84] (A.D. 37-98) at the request of the Roman Emperor, Titus. The complete destruction of the city was quite unexpected, as it was the Roman practice to preserve conquered cities and particularly the temples. The Emperor, Julian the Apostate (361-363 A.D.), tried to rebuild the Temple, so that by re-establishing the Jewish state and the Jewish religion, he might falsify the Christian prophecy. Jews flocked in from every side, and assisted with great enthusiasm in the work. Ammianus Marcellinus, a pagan writer, one of the imperial life-guards, tells us of the issue, one of the most remarkable, as it is one of the best attested events in history:—" [Julian] committed the accomplishment of this task to Alypius of Antioch, who had before that been Lieutenant of Britain. Alypius, therefore, set himself vigorously to the work, and was seconded by the governor of the province. Fearful balls of fire, breaking out near the foundations, continued their attacks, till the workmen, after repeated scorchings, could approach no more; and thus, the fierce elements obstinately repelling them, he gave over his attempt."[85]

C. *Christ Himself the Fulfilment of Prophecy.*—Many Jews were converted by perceiving that in Christ were fulfilled the prophecies about the Messias contained in their sacred books, the books of the Old Testament. We are not here concerned to prove that

---

[81] St. Matt. xiii. 31, 33; xvi. 18.
[82] St. Luke xix. 43, 44.   [83] *id.* xxi. 23,24.
[84] He was a Jew. He first served against the Romans, was taken prisoner and pardoned. He was with Titus at the siege of Jerusalem.
[85] Hist. xxiii. 1-3. See Newman, Essays on Miracles, Sect. vii., p. 334, where several other authorities, Christian and pagan, some of them contemporaries, are quoted.

these books were divinely inspired, nor even that they were authentic. It suffices to accept as true, what no one denies, that the books were in existence long before the birth of Christ.

The religion of the Jews was a religion of expectation, with the belief in a Messias, or a Redeemer to come, as its central doctrine. All that had been foretold of the Redeemer was accurately fulfilled in Christ. The following is a brief summary of the prophetic description of the Redeemer:—He shall be sprung from the line of David (Isaias xi. 1, 2), and shall be born at Bethlehem (Micheas v. 2).[86] He shall be called the Son of God (Ps. ii. 7). He shall judge the poor with justice (Is. xi. 4). His empire shall be multiplied (Is. ix. 7). His Kingdom shall be assailed but shall last for ever (Ps. ii., 1-4). He shall judge all men and crown the just with glory (Is. xxiv., xxviii.). Yet He shall be a man of sorrows, despised and the lowest of men (id. liii.) "He was offered because it was His own will, and He opened not His mouth; He shall be led as a sheep to the slaughter, and shall be dumb as a lamb before His shearer" (id. liii. 7). His hands and feet shall be pierced, His garments shall be divided, and lots cast upon His vesture (Ps. xxi. 17-19). He shall be a light to the Gentiles and bring salvation to the ends of the earth (Is. xlix. 6). "The God of Heaven will set up a Kingdom that shall never be destroyed." (Daniel ii. 44).

It is manifest that the fulfilment of all these prophecies in an individual could not have been due to chance or human contrivance, but must have been the work of God. Christ was therefore the promised Redeemer. But why did not the entire Jewish people perceive that in Christ all prophecy was fulfilled? The question appears to be all the more difficult to answer, when we remember that, as the time of Christ's birth approached, hope in the speedy coming of the Messias had become intense. Reply: (1) The Jewish people at the time of Christ were, as a mass, morally corrupt. Flavius Josephus says that, had not the Romans come to punish them, an earthquake, a deluge, or the lightnings of Sodom would have overwhelmed them. Their wickedness closed their ears to the message of Christ. (2) Their leaders, the Scribes and Pharisees, conceived a terrible hatred against Christ, because He had unsparingly denounced their arrogance and hypocrisy. They were therefore not disposed to examine His claims impartially. (3) Owing partly to the Pharisees' interpretation of the sacred writings, partly to foreign oppression and to national pride, the Jewish people had come to think of the Messias, not as one

---

[86] The chief priests and scribes, in answer to Herod, quoted this text to prove that Christ should be born at Bethlehem.
[87] See Ch. V., Trustworthiness of the Evangelists, 2 (e) end.

who would deliver them from sin, but as a temporal king who would break the Roman yoke and lead them to world-empire. The triumphs of a Spiritual King were all interpreted as the triumphs of an earthly monarch.[87] Even the Apostles could hardly rid themselves of the popular belief, for they asked Christ before His Ascension, with a pathetic yearning for the fulfilment of a patriotic hope, " Lord, wilt Thou at this time again restore the Kingdom of Israel?"[88]

*The Divine origin of Judaism.*—The Divinity of Christ establishes the Divine origin not only of Christianity, but also of the preparatory religion of Judaism. Christ, in His human generation, was a man of the Jewish race. For nearly thirty years He professed and practised the Jewish religion. Therefore, it follows that the Jewish religion was what it claimed to be, a religion given to the Jewish race by God, and that the accounts of all pre-Christian revelation which its sacred books contain must be accepted as of Divine authority.

The Divinity of Christ therefore assures us of His own revelation, and of the revelations given before His time to mankind in general and to the Jewish race in particular.

[Read *Jesus Christ is God*, by P. Courbet, C.T.S., price 7d.; *The Divinity of Christ*, by Rev. Joseph Rickaby, S.J., Sands, price 7d.; also, the excellent work by Rev. P. Finlay, S.J., *The Church of Christ*].

---

[88] Acts i. 6.

# CHAPTER VIII.

## JESUS CHRIST FOUNDED A CHURCH.

*Summary.*

- A. The mission of Christ :—He was sent into the world by His heavenly Father to cleanse all men from sin, to make them children of God and heirs to His Kingdom. These blessings He won, and made accessible to every individual, on condition of faith in His doctrine, obedience to His precepts, and participation in the sacred rites He instituted.
- B. The mission of the Apostles :—Christ preached to but a few. He sent the Apostles to preach to all. He sent them to teach, to govern, and to minister. They obeyed His word.
- C. The foundation of the Church :—Christ, by giving the Apostles this commission, thereby sent them to form a society, His Church.

### A.

**The Mission of Jesus Christ.**—(1) Jesus Christ, the Son of God, was sent into the world by His heavenly Father: "he who honoureth not the Son, honoureth not the Father Who hath sent Him";[1] "Do you say of Him Whom the Father hath sanctified and sent into the world, 'Thou blasphemest,' because I said 'I am the Son of God'?[2] (2) He came to cleanse men from sin: the angel, addressing St. Joseph, said: "She"—the Blessed Virgin—"shall bring forth a Son, and thou shalt call His name Jesus, for He shall save His people from their sins";[3] "the Son of Man is come," He said Himself, "to save that which was lost."[4] He was to save them by His Passion and Death: "the Son of Man [is come] to give His life, a redemption for many";[5] and at the Last Supper He said, taking the chalice, "this is My Blood of the New Testament which shall be shed for many unto the remission of sins."[6] (3) He came, not only to save men from sin, not only to give them life, but to give them a higher and fuller life: "I am come that they may have life and have it more abundantly";[7] He came to make men children of God: "God sent His Son," says St. Paul, "that we might receive the adoption of sons."[8] He came, therefore, to deliver us from sin, and to make us children

---

[1] St. John v. 23.    [2] *id.* x. 36.    [3] St. Matt. i. 21.    [4] *id.* xviii. 11.
[5] *id.* xx. 28.    [6] *id.* xxvi. 28.    [7] St. John x. 10.    [8] Gal. iv. 4.

## JESUS CHRIST FOUNDED A CHURCH.

of God and heirs to His Kingdom. (4) He accomplished His mission: in His prayer to His heavenly Father at the Last Supper, He said: "I have finished the work Thou gavest Me to do."[9] (5) The blessings, viz., remission of sin and Divine sonship, which He purchased for mankind, He has made accessible to all on the following conditions:—(a) that they believe in Him: "This is the will of My Father that sent Me that everyone that seeth the Son and believeth in Him may have life everlasting";[10] "he that believeth not shall be condemned."[11] (b) That they obey His commandments: "You are My friends, if you do the things I command you";[12] "he that loveth Me not, keepeth not My word";[13] (c) that they avail of the sacred rites He instituted: for instance, He says of Baptism, "he that believeth and is baptized shall be saved";[14] "unless a man be born of water and the Holy Ghost he cannot enter into the Kingdom of God";[15] and of the Blessed Eucharist He says, "except you eat the Flesh of the Son of Man and drink His Blood you shall not have life in you."[16]

### B.

**The Mission of the Apostles.** THEIR PREPARATION.—Christ did not Himself teach all men. He taught but a few. These He sent forth to teach all the world what He had taught them. He chose twelve men from among the larger following of His disciples: "He made that twelve should be with Him, and that He might send them forth to preach."[17] For about three years they lived in closest intimacy with Him, and were trained by Him for their future work: "all things whatsoever I have heard of My Father," He said to them, "I have made known to you."[18] Their defects of knowledge or memory were all to be made good: "the Holy Ghost Whom the Father will send in My name, He will teach you all things, and bring all things to your mind, whatsoever I shall have said to you."[19]

I. CHRIST SENT THEM TO TEACH ALL MEN.—He sent them first to the Jews: "Go ye not into the way of the Gentiles . . . but go ye rather to the lost sheep of the house of Israel."[20] Later, He sent them to all mankind. He "died for all."[21] Therefore, He said: "Teach ye all nations";[22] "go ye into the whole world and

---

[9] St. John xvii. 4.  [10] id. vi. 40.
[11] St. Mark xvi. 16.  [12] St. John xv. 14.  [13] id. xiv. 24.
[14] St. Mark xvi. 16.  [15] St. John iii. 5.  [16] id. vi. 54.
[17] St. Mark iii. 14.  [18] St. John xv. 15.  [19] id. xiv. 26.
[20] St. Matt. x. 5, 6.  [21] ii. Cor. v. 15.  [22] St. Matt. xxviii. 19.

preach the Gospel to every creature";[23] "you shall be witnesses for Me in Jerusalem and in all Judaea and Samaria and even unto the uttermost part of the earth."[24] The Apostles obeyed His word, spreading the new message far and wide, so that not many years later St. Paul could say to the Romans that their faith was "spoken of in the whole world."[25] Likewise, he says to the Colossians: "the Gospel which is come unto you, as also it is in the whole world."[26]

II. HE SENT THEM TO GOVERN ALL MEN.—He sent them not only to teach but to govern, *i.e.*, to make laws, to judge, and to punish. For He said to them: "As the Father hath sent Me, so also I send you";[27] "all power is given to Me in heaven and in earth. Going therefore teach ye all nations . . . . and behold I am with you all days even to the consummation of the world."[28] Therefore, Christ clothed His Apostles with His own authority, and promised them unceasing support. What He had been to them, they were to be to the whole world. He had been not only their teacher, but their ruler and master. So, they were to be the rulers and masters of the world. Again, He said to them: "if he"—*i.e.*, the sinner—"will not hear the church, let him be to thee as the heathen and the publican"—*i.e.*, let him be excommunicated—"Amen, I say to you, whatsoever you shall bind on earth shall be bound also in heaven, and whatsoever you shall loose on earth shall be loosed also in heaven,"[29] giving them thereby supreme power in all spiritual matters: their laws, judgments, sentences or remissions would all be ratified and sanctioned in heaven. The Apostles exercised the triple power which He gave them: at the Council of Jerusalem they imposed laws of abstinence on Gentile converts, requiring them to abstain "from things sacrificed to idols, and from blood and from things strangled";[30] St. Paul determines the qualifications of those who should be admitted to Holy Orders;[31] he delivers to the Corinthians a series of precepts and admonitions, ritual, doctrinal, and moral, concluding with the promise that, on coming to them, he would set "the rest in order";[32] he cuts off from the faithful and delivers over to Satan the blasphemers, Hymeneus and Alexander,[33] and the incestuous Corinthian;[34] he instructs Timothy as to the trial of priests, forbidding him to receive an accusation "except under two or three witnesses";[35] he speaks of coming to the Corinthians

---

[23] St. Mark xvi. 15. [24] Acts. i. 8. [25] Rom. i. 8. [26] Col. i. 5, 6.
[27] St. John xx. 21. [28] St. Matt. xxviii. 18-20. [29] *id.* xviii. 18.
[30] Acts xv. 29. [31] i. Tim. iii. 2; Titus i. 6-9. [32] i. Cor. xi. 34; cf. *ibid.* vii., x., xvi. [33] i. Tim. i. 20. [34] i. Cor. v. 1-5.
[35] i. Tim. v. 19.

"with a rod,"[36] and of having the power "in readiness" to punish disobedience.[37]

III. HE SENT THEM TO SANCTIFY MEN BY MEANS OF SACRED RITES.—He bade them administer Baptism: "teach ye all nations, baptizing them in the name of the Father, and of the Son, and of the Holy Ghost."[38] He gave them the power to forgive sins, and, therefore, we must infer that He bade them administer the Sacrament of Penance: "whose sins you shall forgive they are forgiven them, and whose sins you shall retain they are retained";[39] and, after His Resurrection, addressing the Apostles, "He said to them . . . that penance and the remission of sins should be preached in His name unto all nations."[40] He bade them imitate Him in the consecration of bread and wine: "and taking bread He gave thanks, and brake and gave to them saying: This is My Body which is given for you. Do this for a commemoration of Me. In like manner the chalice also . . . saying: This is the chalice, the new testament in My Blood which shall be shed for you."[41] These sacred rites the Apostles administered. We are told, for instance, that they baptized: "they therefore that received his (St. Peter's) word were baptised";[42] that they fed the faithful with the Body and Blood of the Redeemer: "the chalice of benediction which we bless, is it not the communion of the Blood of Christ? And the bread which we break is it not the partaking of the Body of the Lord?"[43]

## C.

**Jesus Christ founded a Society, His Church.**—A society is a number of men united under a common authority for a common object to be attained by common means. In a society, therefore, we distinguish four elements:—there must be (1) a number of men; (2) a common authority binding them together; (3) a common object; and (4) common means for its attainment. We will show that Christ in giving the Apostles their mission sent them to form a religious society, a Church:[44]

(1) CHRIST SENT HIS APOSTLES TO ALL MANKIND. (See above, B. I.)

---

[36] i. Cor. iv. 21.   [37] ii. Cor. x. 6.
[38] St. Matt. xxviii. 19.   [39] St. John xx. 23.   [40] St. Luke xxiv. 47
[41] St. Luke xxii. 19, 20.
[42] Acts ii. 41; cf. viii. 16, 38; ix. 18; x. 48.   [43] i. Cor. x. 16; cf. *ibid*. xi. 27.
[44] "Church" comes from a Greek word, κυριακόν, which means, "belonging to the Lord," *i.e.*, the Lord's House.

(2) HE SENT THEM TO BIND ALL MANKIND UNDER THEIR COMMON AUTHORITY. He did not send them to act independently of one another, but to govern by their collective authority. Had He intended that each of the Apostles should have his own distinct and independent following, He would have founded, not one society, but many societies. But He never spoke of more than one. He always spoke of His *Church*, never of His *churches*: "on this rock I will build My Church."[45] He likened it to "a sheepfold," "a kingdom," "a city," words which imply unity of government or administration. The Apostles themselves regarded the Church as a single society under their collective authority. At the Council of Jerusalem they issued a decree binding men who had been converted by one or other of the Apostles. The Galatians, although the converts of St. Paul, recognized the authority of St. Peter and others of his colleagues, but St. Paul explains to them that he and his fellow Apostles are of one mind.[46] St. Peter, St. Paul, St. John and St. James wrote authoritative letters to communities which had not been converted by them but by other Apostles.[47]

(3) HE SENT THEM TO UNITE MANKIND FOR A COMMON OBJECT.—The object of His society was manifestly the object for which He had come into the world, viz., to cleanse men from sin, to make them holy, to make them children of God and heirs to His Kingdom. He and His Apostles were one in purpose: "As the Father hath sent Me, so also I send you."

(4) THE OBJECT WAS TO BE ATTAINED BY THE EMPLOYMENT OF COMMON MEANS.—The members of His society were to attain their object by the use of the same common means, viz., by believing His doctrine, by obeying His commandments, and by availing of the sacred rites instituted by Him for their sanctification.

*It must be carefully noted that in these Chapters (VIII., IX.) we are speaking of the nature and characteristics of the Church which Christ founded. In Chapter X. we show which one of the existing churches can lawfully claim to be identical with it.*

---

[45] St. Matt xvi. 18. "The Church is One."   [46] Gal. i. and ii.   [47] See Ch. IX.,

## CHAPTER IX.

THE CHARACTERISTICS OF THE CHURCH OF CHRIST.

THE CHURCH, AN ARGUMENT FOR HIS DIVINITY.

*Summary.*

    *A.* The Church of Christ is (I.) *imperishable, Apostolic,* (II.) *one, universal* or *Catholic* (membership, therefore, obligatory on all), *visible, holy,* (III.) *infallible.*

    *B.* An argument for the Divinity of Christ from the rapid propagation of Christianity, and from the constancy of the martyrs.

    **N.B.**—*Read the note at the end of preceding Chapter.*

### *A.*
### I.

THE CHURCH IS IMPERISHABLE AND APOSTOLIC.

**The Church is Imperishable.**—Christ willed that this society, His Church, should be imperishable, that it should last to the end of the world, teaching, governing, and sanctifying men. "I say to thee," He said to St. Peter, "thou art Peter"—*i.e.*, a rock—"and on this rock I will build My Church and the gates of hell shall not prevail against it."[1] "The gates of hell," that is, death, destruction, the power of its enemies. Again, He sent His Apostles to preach to "every creature," to "all nations," and encouraged them with the promise: "Behold, I am with you all days even to the consummation of the world."[2] Had Christ intended that His Church should last only for a time, He would have set forth in clear prophecy the signs of its dissolution. The termination of a Divine institution should, we may confidently assert, be as marvellous and as manifest as its beginning.

**The Church is Apostolic.**—By saying that the Church is Apostolic we mean that in every age the rulers of the

---

[1] St. Matt. xvi. 18.      [2] *id.* xxviii. 20.

Church are clothed in the authority given by Christ to the Apostles. The word "apostolic" has other senses also with which we are not at present concerned. Christ said to the Apostles: "as the Father hath sent Me, I also send you";[3] "all power is given to Me in heaven and in earth. Going, therefore, teach ye all nations . . . and behold I am with you all days even to the consummation of the world."[4] Christ by these words placed the Apostles in charge of a work which will not be completed until the world ends. The Apostles themselves are dead, yet according to the terms of Christ's assurance they must in some sense remain in the world until the end of time. They can remain in the world only through representatives chosen in the manner which they themselves prescribed. They must, therefore, have made provision that their authority should be passed on to others and transmitted down the whole line of their successors, so that, in every generation, the rulers of the Church could say :—" Our authority is the authority of the Apostles, for we are one with them by lawful succession." The words of Christ make it clear that the Apostles are the last envoys whom God will send to the human race. The authority which He gave them and their successors He will never give to any others. The mission of the Apostles is final and perpetual. That the Apostles did actually make provision for their succession can be proved by many authorities, *e.g.*, St. Clement, who died about 100 A.D., says : " Christ was sent by God, the Apostles by Christ. They appointed bishops and deacons . . . (and) they made order that when they (the bishops and deacons) died, other men of tried virtue should succeed to their ministry";[5] and St. Irenaeus, writing towards the end of the second century, speaks of " the bishops and their successors down to our own time who have been appointed by the Apostles."[6]

---

[3] St. John xx. 21.  [4] St. Matt. xxviii. 18-20.
[5] i. Clem. xlii., xliv.  [6] Adv. Haer. Book iii., ch. 8.

*THE CHARACTERISTICS OF THE CHURCH OF CHRIST.*

II.

THE CHURCH OF CHRIST IS ONE, UNIVERSAL, VISIBLE, AND HOLY.

The fourfold proposition that the Church founded by Christ is one, universal, visible, and holy, has been already implicitly established in the course of our proof that the Church is a society. But a more detailed and explicit treatment is necessary.

**The Church is One.**—*Particular proof of the unity of the Church.* THE CHURCH IS ONE IN GOVERNMENT.—This particular proposition has been already proved (p. 78). To recapitulate :—(1) Christ spoke of His *Church*, not of His *Churches*. Therefore, He meant that His Church should be one society under one government, not several societies, each under its own government, distinct and separate from the rest. (2) He compared His Church to a "sheepfold," "a city," "a kingdom," thereby implying unity of government. (3) The Apostles themselves regarded the Church as one in government. Further proofs :— (4) When Christ was founding His Church, He said to the Apostles, "as the Father hath sent Me, so also I send you."[7] The Apostles were to take the place of Christ in the world; they were to act as though they were not many but one, as though they, collectively, were the one Christ Himself; they were, therefore, to govern the Church with one, undivided authority. (5) The Church, St. Paul says, must be "one body and one Spirit."[8] It must be like the living body; and, as, in the living body, there is but one governing will, so in the Church there must be but one governing authority

THE CHURCH IS ONE IN FAITH.—(1) Christ said to the Apostles: "Teach ye all nations . . . teaching them

---
[7] St. John xx. 21.   [8] Eph. iv. 4.

to observe *all* things whatsoever I have commanded you."[9] The Apostles, therefore, were to teach every man the whole doctrine of Christ. They were to insist that every man should believe one and the same body of truths. The Church of Christ, therefore, must be one in faith. (2) In the Church, according to St. Paul, there must be "one Lord, one faith, one baptism."[10] The Church, he says, in the simile he so often repeats, is a living body; and, as, in the living body, there is but one mind, so in the Church there must be but one faith. The faithful, he says to the Romans, "with one mind and with one mouth" are to "glorify God and the Father of Our Lord, Jesus Christ."[11] "I beseech you, brethren," he says to the Corinthians, "by the name of Our Lord Jesus Christ, that you all speak the same thing, and that there be no schisms among you, but that you be perfect in the same mind, and in the same judgment."[12] "Mark them who make dissensions and offences contrary to the doctrines which you have learnt, and avoid them, for they that are such serve not Christ Our Lord."[13]

THE CHURCH IS ONE IN WORSHIP.—The proposition follows directly from the preceding. Worship is nothing more than a practical manifestation of faith. The members of the Church are one in faith; they must, therefore, be one also in worship. Their unity of faith excludes the possibility of any disagreement among them as to the rites by which God is to be adored and man sanctified. Note that, of the three species of unity, unity of faith is the chief. It is, as it were, the root of the other two. Converts to Christianity believed first of all in Christ and His doctrine. Believing His doctrine, they believed, as part of it, that they were bound to worship God in the manner prescribed by Him and to yield obedience to the superiors whom He had appointed for their guidance.

---

[9] St. Matt. xxviii. 19, 20.    [10] Eph. iv. 5.    [11] Rom. xv. 6.
[12] i. Cor. i. 10.    [13] Rom. xvi. 17, 18.

*General proof of the unity of the Church.*—Christ, in His prayer after the last Supper, said: " not for them only "—*i.e.*, His Apostles—" do I pray, but for them also who through their word shall believe in Me, that they all may be one, as Thou, Father, in Me, and I in Thee; that they, also, may be one in Us."[14] Christ, therefore, desired for His Church an absolute unity, a unity which should exclude all division, whether in government, doctrine, or worship, for He likens it to the perfect unity of the Father and His Divine Son. St. Paul is of one mind with His Lord and Master. He holds that unity is the fundamental characteristic of the Church. Over and over again, as we have said, he compares the Church to a living body: "as the body is one and has many members, and all the members of the body, whereas they are many, yet are one body, so also is Christ. For, in one Spirit were we all baptized into one body, whether Jew or Gentile."[15] He conceives the members of the Church as parts of the same living organism. Vivified by the same spiritual life, they believe the same doctrine, they participate in the same worship, and yield obedience to one and the same authority.

**The Church is Universal or Catholic. The Obligation of Membership.** THE CHURCH IS UNIVERSAL OR CATHOLIC. —Christ gave His Apostles a most emphatic command not to confine their teaching to the men of any particular race or social status. He bade them preach the Gospel to " all nations "[16] and to " every creature."[17] The Apostles obeyed Him: St. Paul applies to himself and his fellow preachers the words of the Psalmist, " their sound hath gone forth into all the earth, and their words unto the ends of the whole world,"[18] and he tells the Colossians that the Gospel is

---

[14] St. John xvii. 20, 21.  [15] i. Cor. xii. 12f.  cf. Eph. i., v.; Rom. xii. See Mgr. Benson's *Christ in the Church*.
[16] St Matt. xxviii. 19.  [17] St. Mark xvi. 15.  [18] Rom. ix. 18.

believed " in the whole world."[19] The Apostle, we must understand, is speaking, not of an absolute, but of a moral catholicity, *i.e.*, of a membership which, in kind and extent, could be described as catholic or universal in the ordinary speech of men. The moral catholicity of the Church is both social and numerical : it is social, in the sense that the membership of the Church includes men of every condition and grade of culture; it is numerical, in the sense that the Church is widely diffused throughout the world. The Church could not have failed to achieve, within a reasonable time after her foundation, a moral catholicity, because her teachers were supported by Christ Himself in their mission to the world, and because her doctrines, being the doctrines of God, must have made a powerful appeal to the reason and the heart of all well-disposed men. Since the Church of Christ, being imperishable, still exists in the world, it must, for the same reasons, viz., Divine aid and suitability of doctrine to human needs, possess a moral catholicity; and it must, moreover, in accordance with the will of Christ that all men be saved, strive by practical and organized effort for the ideal of absolute universality.

THE OBLIGATION OF MEMBERSHIP.—The command of Christ to the Apostles to preach the Gospel to " every creature " implies a corresponding obligation on the part of all men to hear and obey them, and, therefore, to become members of the Church : "preach the Gospel to every creature," said Christ, ". . . . he that believeth not shall be condemned."[20] No man, therefore, who, on coming to know the true Church, refuses to join it can be saved. Neither can he be saved, if, having once entered the Church, he forsake it through heresy or schism : " a man that is a heretic, after the first and second admonition, avoid, knowing that he that is such

---

[19] Col. i. 6. See Ch. VIII. B.I. [20] St. Mark xvi. 15, 16.

an one is subverted and sinneth, being condemned by his own judgment."[21] The Church, as St. Paul says, is the living body whereof Christ is the Head. He who severs himself from the Church, severs himself from Christ, and cannot be saved, for in Christ alone is salvation: "I am the vine," said Christ, "you the branches: he that abideth in Me, and I in him, the same beareth much fruit, for without Me you can do nothing. If any one abide not in Me, he shall be cast forth. . . . . They shall gather him up, and cast him into the fire and he burneth."[22]

**The Church is Visible.**—Christ established the Church as a visible society, that is, as a society which stood out plainly before the eyes of men as an organized body, consisting of teachers and taught, rulers and subjects, who joined in public worship and made open profession of their belief. The Apostles admitted men to membership of the Church by the public rite of Baptism; they made laws affecting the external behaviour of the faithful, and they exacted obedience; they gave the faithful the command of Christ to confess their faith openly: "everyone therefore that shall confess Me before men, I will also confess him before My Father who is in heaven. But he that shall deny Me before men, I will also deny him before My Father who is in heaven."[23]

**The Church is Holy.**—THE CHURCH IS HOLY IN HER FOUNDER.—God Himself is the founder of the Church, the Author of her organization and all her work. She is holy, therefore, in her system of government, in her doctrine, in her worship and in her object.

THE CHURCH IS HOLY IN HER DOCTRINE.—Non-believers admit the excellence of Christ's moral precepts of which,

---
[21] Titus iii. 10.  [22] St. John xv. 5, 6. See Ch. VIII. B.II.
[23] St. Matt x. 32.

as of all His teaching, the Church is the custodian. Not content with the common virtues, such as truthfulness and honesty, which are practised by many pagans, He urged His followers to higher things. He bade them strive to attain the ideals of heroic virtue. He recommended to them fraternal charity, meekness, and self-denial in its various forms, *e.g.*, voluntary poverty, submission to persecution, self-sacrifice even unto death to testify to their faith or to relieve the sufferings and save the souls of others.[24] He summed up all these ideals in one: "Be ye perfect, as also your heavenly Father is perfect."[25]

THE CHURCH IS HOLY IN HER MEMBERS.—Christ did not demand such perfection of every member of His Church, nor did He say that all its members, high and low, would be holy, even in the humblest sense of the word: man may abuse the liberty God has given him, and choose evil instead of good. So, we find that among the Apostles, who had lived in intimate friendship with God Himself, there was a traitor; so, we find that Christ likens His Kingdom (Church) to a net that enmeshes worthless fish as well as good,[26] or to a field wherein the cockle grows among the wheat.[27] Still, Christ meant that His Church, as a whole, would at all times be remarkable for sanctity and would exhibit many instances of the realization of the highest ideals. His Church is "the good tree" that "bringeth forth good fruit."[28] She must needs bring forth the good fruit of virtue, for Christ, her Founder, Who is God Himself, will be always with her.

HER SANCTITY PROVED BY MIRACLES.—He will never cease to prove her sanctity by miracles, for He said: "These signs shall follow them that believe: In My

---

[24] Read the Sermon on the Mount, St. Matt. v., vi., vii.
[25] *id.* v. 48.
[26] St. Matt. xiii. 24-30.   [27] *id.* xiii. 47, 48.   [28] *id.* vii. 17.

name they shall cast out devils; they shall speak with new tongues; they shall take up serpents; and if they shall drink any deadly thing, it shall not hurt them; they shall lay their hands upon the sick, and they shall recover";[29] "he that believeth in Me, the works that I do, he also shall do, and greater than these shall he do."[30]

### III
### THE CHURCH IS INFALLIBLE.

The Church is infallible, that is, the Church cannot err in teaching and interpreting, as of faith, the truths which Christ delivered to her keeping. (1) Indirect Proof: If it be admitted that the Church can err in exacting the assent of faith for her doctrine, it follows (a) that God has bound men on pain of damnation to believe what is false: " He that believeth not," He said, " will be condemned";[31] and (b) that there can be no certainty whether any particular doctrine is the doctrine of God. (2) Proof from Imperishability: The Church will never perish. She will always teach men with Divine authority. Hence, she can never err in her teaching. (3) Proof from Unity of Faith: The Church must at all times teach and believe the same body of Divine truths. Possessing unity of faith, she must possess, also, the means by which that unity may be preserved and defended. Owing to the waywardness or wickedness of men, the plainest doctrines of Christianity are liable, as we know from history, to constant misinterpretation. There is always a danger that error may creep into the Church, and error would be fatal to unity. The Church must, therefore, be

---
[29] St. Mark xvi. 17, 18.    [30] St. John xiv. 12.
[31] St. Mark xvi. 16.

empowered by God to declare with an infallible voice whether a doctrine has been revealed or not, and to expel from her fold and threaten with damnation all who dispute her decision.

We distinguish "the Church teaching" and "the Church believing." By "the Church teaching" we mean the teachers of the Church, considered, not individually, but collectively; by "the Church believing" we mean the general mass of the faithful. "The Church teaching," we say, is infallible; so, also, "the Church believing." The infallibility of the former is called active; the infallibility of the latter, passive. Those in whom infallibility, whether active or passive, resides, are called the "subject of Infallibility." The doctrines in regard to which the Church, whether "teaching" or "believing," is infallible constitute what is termed the "object of Infallibility." The object of Infallibility consists of:—(a) all doctrines in the Deposit of Faith, i.e., all doctrines delivered by Christ to the Apostles; they are the sum of His public revelation to mankind; any subsequent revelations which God may have been pleased to grant are private, and form no part of the Deposit of Faith; (b) all doctrines, or statements, which, though not found in the Deposit of Faith, are necessary for its safe custody, e.g., that a certain book contains heretical teaching. The Deposit of Faith comprises all doctrines found in the Bible and in Tradition. (1) The Bible consists of the inspired[32] books of the Old and the New Testament; God Himself is its author. (2) Tradition embraces all those truths which, though never committed to writing under Divine inspiration, have been handed down within the Church from age to age in various ways; many of them are found, e.g., in the works of the Fathers of the Church, those learned and saintly ecclesiastical writers who lived before 600 A.D., or in the Acts of the Martyrs, which record in several instances the express doctrines for which the martyrs suffered; many of them, in the teaching of Popes and Councils; many of them, also, are attested by early paintings and inscriptions, found in the Catacombs and elsewhere, or by the practices and customs of the Universal Church. Catholics call the Bible and Tradition "the sources of Faith."

*Since the Church founded by Christ is imperishable, it exists in the world at the present day clothed in all its attributes. It is Apostolic, one, catholic, visible, holy, and infallible.*

---

[32] For definition of inspiration, see Ch. XI. E., first paragraph.

## B.

## ARGUMENT FOR THE DIVINITY OF CHRIST FROM THE RAPID PROPAGATION OF CHRISTIANITY AND THE FORTITUDE OF THE MARTYRS.

Tacitus says[33] that in the first persecution of the Church (64-68 A.D.) under Nero " a vast multitude of Christians " were put to death. Fifty years later, Pliny,[34] the Propraetor of Bithynia in Asia Minor, reports to the Emperor Trajan that he is startled and perplexed by the number, influence, and pertinacity of the Christians he finds in his district and in the neighbouring province of Pontus. St. Justin Martyr writing about 150 A.D., says : " There is no race of men, barbarian or Greek, nay, of those who live in waggons or who are shepherds or nomads in tents among whom prayers and eucharists are not offered to the Father and Maker of the Universe through the name of the crucified Jesus."[35] At the conversion of the Emperor Constantine in 324 A.D., about one-twelfth of the Roman world was Christian. The proportion had risen to one-half about the year 400 A.D. Three decades later an imperial document declared that paganism had almost completely disappeared. The triumph of the new creed was social as well as numerical. Gradually it had worked its way upwards from despised toilers to proud officials, from ignorant Jews to learned philosophers. Such a rapid and world-wide revolution cannot be explained by natural causes :—(1) The founder of the religion was, in the eyes of the world, a poor Galilean tradesman. Four of His Apostles were fishermen, and one a petty tax-collector. When SS. Peter and John, after the first Christian miracle, were arraigned before the Council, wonder was expressed that they, being " illiterate and

---

[33] *Annals* xv. 44. Tacitus (55-120 A.D. approx.)  [34] Lib. x. Ep. 97
[35] Dial. cum Tryph. n. 117.

ignorant men,"[36] had the presumption to preach a new Gospel. The same charge was repeated many times in the years that followed. "Christians," said their opponents, "are fools ... the lowest dregs of the people ... unpolished boors, ignorant even of the sordid arts of life; they do not understand even civil matters, how can they understand Divine? ... They have left their tongs, mallets, and anvils to preach about the things of heaven."[37] Such was the character the Christian teachers bore. Against them were pitted the power, wealth, and intelligence of the Roman Empire. (2) The doctrine preached by the Apostles was new and repellent to the worldly-minded. It demanded faith and humble submission, brotherly love and self-sacrifice unto death, from a people sunk in materialism, lustful, proud, revengeful, and almost incapable of any elevated concept of the Deity. It urged them to smash to pieces the long hallowed images of gods that were nothing more, they were now told, than personifications of the powers of nature and of base, human passions. It bade them forsake their ancient religion, so flattering to the senses, with its noble temples, its stately ritual, its days of public amusement, and attach themselves to a joyless band of despicable men whose eyes were fixed on the things of another world and who bowed down in worship before the image of a crucified malefactor.

But, it may be objected, perhaps the very corruption of the world at the time made men sick of vice and long for a great moral reform. We reply: (1) that at Rome in those days the Stoic philosophers taught a very pure system of morals, and yet they made no impression on the masses; (2) that admiration for Christian morals is very far removed from full faith in Christian teaching and from the practice of

---

[36] Acts iv. 13. [37] For references, see Newman, *Grammar of Assent*. p. 468

Christian precepts; (3) that we cannot conceive how, without the grace of the Holy Spirit, men could ever have overcome their repugnance for what must have seemed the unspeakable folly or blasphemy of its central doctrine that a Galilean workman was the Son of God. But, again, it may be urged that the rapid propagation of Christianity can be explained by the ease and security with which men could travel in those days to all parts of the Roman Empire. We reply: (1) that other religions, *e.g.*, the worship of Mithra and Isis, enjoyed similar facilities, and yet failed to win and retain worldwide acceptance; (2) that while Roman roads and Roman security on land and sea helped to speed the Christian messenger to the furthest limits of the earth, all such advantages were far more than countervailed by the edge of the Roman sword; ten times, that vast empire concentrated all its might on the destruction of the infant Church, and ten times the followers of the poor Galilean emerged triumphant.

The persecution of Christianity, in its severity and duration, in the number, quality, and fortitude of its victims forms a unique episode in history. The hostility of the Empire, never dormant for three centuries, broke out with especial violence on ten separate occasions. "The very young and the very old, the child,[38] the youth in the heyday of his passions, the sober man of middle age, maidens and mothers of families, boors and slaves as well as philosophers and nobles, solitary confessors and companies of men and women—all these were seen equally to defy the powers of darkness to do their worst .... They faced the implements of torture as the soldier takes his place before the enemy's battery. They cheered and ran forward to meet his attack, and, as it were, dared

---

[38] On *child-martyrs*, see Devas, *The Key to the World's Progress*, p. 74, Longmans, Green, price 7d.

him, if he would, to destroy the numbers who kept closing up the foremost rank, as their comrades who had filled it fell."[39] But their courage was not as the courage of a hardened soldier; he has been trained to valour; he goes into battle, not as a lamb to the slaughter, not as a passive victim merely to suffer and to die, but with weapons in his hands, prepared to give blow for blow; and in fulfilling his duty he is supported by the conviction that to stand his ground is safer than to retreat, or by shame of cowardice, or by desire to win the applause of men; whereas the martyrs, from the world's standpoint, had everything to lose and nothing to gain from their fortitude; they—many of them no more than poor little children—suffered themselves to be smeared with pitch and set alight, to be flung into boiling cauldrons, to be torn to pieces by the beasts of the amphitheatre, and all this amid the execrations of the crowd who cursed their obstinacy and promised them every reward, if they would but yield. All their strength came from the one Thought, the one Image of their Crucified Saviour Whom they loved with an impassioned love. But how, without the inspiration of God, could that same Thought have "entered into myriads of men, women, and children of all ranks, especially the lower, and have had the power to wean them from their indulgences and sins, and to nerve them against the most cruel tortures, and to last in vigour as a sustaining influence for seven or eight generations, till . . . it broke the obstinacy of the strongest and wisest government which the world has ever seen?"[40]

To put the whole argument briefly:—The rapid propagation of Christianity among all classes throughout the world was miraculous, (1) because its preachers were men of no worldly influence; (2) because its chief doctrine was strange and repellent, while its system of

---
[39] Newman, *Grammar of Assent*, pp. 477-8.
[40] *Id. ibid.* p. 465.

morals was severe and offered no bribe to human infirmity; (3) because it was resisted by all the power of the Roman Empire. The fortitude of the Martyrs was miraculous, (1) because vast numbers of every rank and age, including children of tender years, suffered; (2) because their constancy was proof against the most terrible tortures; (3) because they were unmoved in face of the attractive rewards promised them, if they yielded; (4) because the persecutions extended over three centuries. God, therefore, proved by miracles that Christianity was a true religion. Christ, its Founder, was, therefore, as He claimed, the Son of God, equal to His Father.

# CHAPTER X.

THE IDENTIFICATION OF THE CHURCH OF CHRIST.

THE CATHOLIC CHURCH IS THE TRUE CHURCH.

*Summary* :—

I. The true Church must have all the following marks:—
   (1) it must claim Infallibility;
   (2) it must claim Apostolicity;
   (3) it must be universal and one—one in government, faith, and worship;
   (4) it must be holy.

II. A. The false Christian Churches:—
   1. Protestantism : its origin; its doctrines. It has none of the marks of the true Church.
   2. The Schismatic Greek Church : its origin; its doctrine. It has not all the marks of the true Church.
   3. The Branch Theory, viz., that the true Church consists of the Church of England, the Schismatic Greek Church, and the Catholic Church—Rejected, because destructive of unity.
   
   B. The Catholic Church alone has all the marks of the true Church.
   
   C. Her miraculous vitality. In itself a sufficient proof that she is the true Church.

III. The chief non-Christian religions.

## I.

**Method of Identification.**—The Church of Christ, being imperishable, exists in the world at the present day. We are bound under grave obligation to be members of it. We know its characteristics, and are, therefore, able to identify it[1] :—(1) it must claim infallibility; (2) it must claim Apostolicity; (3) it must be universal and, at the

---

[1] As marks of identity, however, some of these characteristics are more telling than others. In the last Chapter, we arranged them in a logical order, developing them from the two main propositions, that the Church is a society, founded by Christ, and that she is imperishable; in this, we take them in the order of evidential value, omitting those which are less important for our present purpose.

same time, one—one in government, faith, and worship; (4) it must be holy. A church which does not possess *all* these marks or characteristics cannot be the Church of Christ.

**The Divisions of Christianity.—Our Line of Proof.**—In the world of to-day, those who believe in the Divinity of Christ and profess to be members of His Church fall into three divisions, viz., Protestants, Schismatic Greeks, and Catholics. Which of these groups is the Church of Christ? Or, does it consist of some combination of the three? These are the questions which we now purpose answering. We will show that neither the Protestant nor the Schismatic Greek Church, nor a combination of Protestants, Schismatic Greeks, and Catholics can claim to be the Church of Christ. When we have established so much, we have proved by a negative argument, *i.e.*, by the method of rejection, that the Catholic Church must be the true Church. We then proceed to show that she does actually bear all the marks detailed in the preceding paragraph. We conclude with a distinct proof from her miraculous vitality, as evidenced in the survival of the Papacy through all the centuries down to the present day, in spite of assaults to which a merely human dynasty must have succumbed.

## II.

### A.—THE FALSE CHRISTIAN CHURCHES.

#### § 1.

**Protestantism.** Its Divisions.—The Protestant sects include the Lutherans of North Germany, Denmark, Norway, and Sweden; the Presbyterians (Calvinists) of Switzerland, Holland, Scotland, North-East of Ireland, and North America; the Church of England, Methodism, and an ever increasing number of smaller associations.

Its Origin.—The Reformation, as the Protestant movement is inaccurately termed, began in Germany in the sixteenth century, and spread thence to Switzerland, France, the Netherlands, Denmark and Norway, Sweden, and England. The following were the chief causes of the success of the Reformation:—(a) *The unhappy state of religion at this period*: The numerous richly endowed offices in the Church had attracted unworthy men to her ministry; in many countries, she had become the slave of royal power; even the Papacy itself was for a time in bondage to the crown of France; the loyalty of men had been much weakened by a disastrous schism (The Great Western Schism, 1378-1417) during which there were two, and, for a short period, three rival Popes; many grave abuses, not, however, at all so grave as the enemies of the Church represented, had arisen in connection with the levying of Papal monies; in general, there was much laxity of discipline, and so, in the hour of stress, the Church in many places found herself with bitter enemies in her household and with too few zealous defenders. (b) *Political considerations*: In Germany, the princes thought that by joining in a religious insurrection they might succeed in casting off the yoke of the Emperor,[2] who, they knew, would unquestionably defend the old faith. Their designs naturally met with much encouragement in France, where the Emperor's power was a cause of uneasiness. Further, the German princes and with them the king of the united countries, Denmark and Norway, and the king of Sweden were attracted by the Lutheran doctrine that the king is head of the Church in his own dominions, since it enabled them to consolidate their power and seize the vast wealth of ecclesiastical corporations. While Lutheranism favoured the pretensions of kings, Calvinism, on the other hand, with its denial of royal supremacy and its republican spirit, was of service in what may be described as the anti-monarchical, or anti-imperial, struggle of the Swiss and the people of the Netherlands. In England, Henry VIII. regarded the Papal supremacy as an obstacle to his lust and rapacity, and used the great power of the crown to effect a schism; during the reigns of Edward VI. and Elizabeth, the doctrines of Luther and Calvin were introduced so that, by a complete separation from Rome in obedience and faith, all foreign interference in the affairs of the kingdom might be permanently excluded. (c) *The popular character of its doctrines:* The doctrines of the Reformers offered an easy remedy for sin, abolished all irksome duties such as fasting and confession, and flattered national and personal vanity, by denying the authority of the Pope, and by investing the individual with the power of choosing and interpreting his own faith. (d) *Humanism or the Revival of Learning:* Humanism, though

---

[2] Charles V (1519-56), King of Spain and Emperor of Germany. The Netherlands and parts of Italy also belonged to his dominions.

favoured by many learned Catholics, and patronized by Popes, caused a ferment of intellectual unrest throughout Europe. It prepared the minds of men to admit novelties in faith as willingly as they had admitted them in the department of secular knowledge. (e) *The personality of Luther*: Luther (1483-1546), the leader of the revolt, was a man of great natural ability. He had all the qualities of a successful demagogue—vast energy, effrontery, coarseness of manner, power of invective, quick wit, cutting sarcasm, an unrivalled grasp of popular and forceful diction, fanaticism, fractiousness, and utter want of self-restraint. His imperfect theological training, his ignorance of the early history of the Church, his incapacity for exact reasoning, all these defects, while they helped to blind him to his iniquity, have left their clear imprint on the illogical system of doctrine which he constructed. —Luther opened hostilities in 1517 by denouncing a Papal proclamation which granted an indulgence, on the usual conditions of confession and communion, to all who should assist by their contributions, or, by their prayers, if they were too poor to contribute, in the charitable work of rebuilding St. Peter's, Rome. Although the object was worthy of the support of Christendom, the Pope found himself heir to the dissatisfaction created by his predecessors' exactions and misapplications of Church monies. Luther, at first, had the sympathy of some well-meaning men, but lost it as soon as he showed that his design was not reformation but destruction. His movement threatened at one time to overrun all Europe with the exception of Italy, Spain, and Portugal. A reaction, however, set in which wrested from it half its triumphs, and pressed it back to those Teutonic areas from which, we may say, it has not since advanced. At the Council of Trent, where the true reformation took place, the Church cast the slough of abuses, and in a brief time, through the zeal of her missionaries, repaired her losses in the Old World by successes in the New. It cannot be said that Luther[2a] and his associates were actuated by piety or by zeal for religion. Most of them, in fact, were men of loose morals, remarkable even in that corrupt age for profligacy, and not one of them could make any claim whatsoever to sanctity.

ITS DOCTRINES.—The following are the chief tenets of Luther: (1) the Bible privately interpreted is the sole rule of faith; (2) man is made holy by faith alone without good works; his soul is always in the state of sin: faith does not remove sin, but merely hides it from the eyes of God; man's will is not free; (3) the Church is invisible,[2b] although individual congregations are visible; all believers are equally priests, and need no special spiritual power to act as pastors or presbyters; the State has supreme power in all

---

[2a] See Grisar's *Life of Luther*.    [2b] *i.e.* it consists of the just alone.

church appointments; (4) there are three sacraments, viz., Baptism, Eucharist, and Penance, but they do not confer grace in the Catholic sense. Calvin (1509-64) agreed with Luther as to (1), but added to (2) that man is predestined by God, independently of his own acts, to salvation or perdition; he also held that (3) the Church is visible,[2c] and independent of the State; presbyters elected by the people thereby receive the spiritual authority of bishops; (4) the Lutheran list of sacraments must be reduced to two, viz., Baptism and the Eucharist.—It would be impossible to give a brief and clear account of all the extraordinary vicissitudes through which Protestant doctrine has passed from its origin down to the present time. A great number of German Lutherans now hold that Christ founded no Church, that religious belief is a matter of private opinion, or sentiment, and may be quite false. In the official Protestant Church of England we may identify three parties, viz., the Ritualist, which believes in the Divine institution and authority of bishops, holds almost all the doctrines of Catholicism with the exception of the Infallibility and Primacy of the Pope, and claims Apostolic succession; the Evangelical, which is tinged with Calvinism; and the Rationalist, which regards the Divinity of Christ and the Trinity as debatable points.

**The Protestant Church is not the true Church.**—Protestantism, as a doctrinal system, is perhaps the weakest heresy ever proposed. It has not even one of the essential marks of the true Church. (1) It repudiates all claim to infallibility. Confessedly, therefore, it may teach false doctrine, and can be no guide to truth. It leaves the ultimate decision on every point to the individual judgment. (2) It does not claim to be Apostolic.[3] Neither Luther nor Calvin received lawful appointment to teach. Luther, indeed, appears to have claimed a direct commission from God Himself,[4] but, needless to say, his pretension was not supported by miracles. (3) It is not catholic, either socially or numerically. Not socially, because the religion is practically confined to portions of the Teutonic races. Nor numerically, because the total of its adherents is about 170 millions, divided up into over 100 independent sects, each of which must be regarded as a separate church.[5]—If, as may be asserted, those 170 millions really form but one church, then that church has not the unity of

---

[2c] He also believed in an invisible Church consisting of the elect alone.

[3] Some members of the Anglican Church claim that it is Apostolic. See below § 3 The Branch Theory and B II.

[4] He said he was the instrument of God, chosen to reform the Church which had been corrupted since Apostolic times. Kirchenlex, viii., 325, 2nd ed. [5] See below B. III, footnote.

the Church of Christ. It is notoriously not one either in government, faith, or worship. Its tenet that private judgment is the final arbiter of faith is a principle of destruction, ever creating new sects, and ever making the entire Protestant following more and more unlike the one, living body of Christ, the true Church. (4) It is not holy in the sense explained in the preceding chapter. Its denial of free-will and human responsibility undermines all morality. There are, of course, many Protestants who lead most upright lives, but their probity is due, not to the principles of Protestantism, but to good traditions inherited from Catholicism. —In recent times, some praiseworthy efforts have been made by English Protestants, in spite of much official discouragement, to imitate the Catholic religious communities in their practice of the heroic virtues.—If Protestantism as such had any power to make men holy, we should expect to find a pre-eminent degree of sanctity in its founders and chief promoters. But enthusiasm itself has failed to detect such a quality in Luther, Calvin, Henry VIII., or Elizabeth.

The doctrine of the Reformers that the Bible, privately interpreted, is the sole rule of faith, *i.e.*, that it is the one and only sure and easy means of determining what we should believe, implies (1) that all truths necessary for salvation are found in the Bible, and (2) that everyone can ascertain, and ought to ascertain, those truths for himself by reading the Bible. As to (1), the Bible cannot be the only store-house of Divine truth for the following reasons:—(*a*) The Bible itself says nothing of the kind. It says, in fact, the contrary. St. Paul writes: "Therefore, brethren, stand fast, and hold the traditions which you have learned whether *by word* or by an epistle."[6] And St. John says in his Gospel: "But there are also many other things which Jesus did, which, if they were written, every one, the world itself, I think, would not be able to contain the books that should be written."[7] (*b*) Christ did not send the Apostles to write but to preach. (*c*) The New Testament did not begin to come into existence for two or three decades after the Ascension.—As to (2): (*a*) Christ never said that a knowledge of letters was necessary for salvation. He never commanded us to discover by reading the Bible what we should believe. Such a command would have been a grievous hardship at a time when there were no printed books. (*b*) The Bible itself gives us no satisfactory proof of its inspiration or account of its contents. We require some living authority to say to us: "This book, consisting of such and such parts, has God for its author." The book itself cannot say this. (*c*) The Bible refers to its own obscurity: St. Peter says that in the epistles of

---

[6] 2 Thess. ii. 14.     [7] xxi. 25.

St. Paul there are "certain things hard to be understood which the unlearned and the unstable wrest, as they do also the other scriptures, to their own destruction."[8] (d) The practical proof of the insufficiency of the Bible as a rule of faith is the diversity of belief among Protestants, every extravagance of doctrine being professedly based on some one's interpretation of the sacred text. —The Catholic Rule of Faith is the teaching authority of the Church.

The substitution of private judgment for a living infallible teaching authority is the root-error of Protestantism. Its destructive force is seen, not only in the multiplication of sects, but in the denial of the Divinity of Christ, the inspiration of the Scriptures, and other doctrines, regarded by the early Reformers as fundamental.

§ 2.

**The Schismatic Greek Church.** ITS DIVISIONS.—The Schismatic Greek Church consists of several independent churches, viz., the Patriarchates of Constantinople, Alexandria, Antioch, and Jerusalem, the Churches of Russia, Greece, Roumania, Serbia, Bulgaria, Montenegro and five others.

ITS ORIGIN.—The separation of the Greek Church from the Roman Catholic Church was due (a) to the ancient rivalry of Greek and Latin; (b) to the pride and ambition of the Patriarchs of Constantinople, who saw in the transfer (330 A.D.) of the Emperor's seat of residence from Rome to Constantinople a ground for proclaiming their release from the supreme authority of the Pope; (c) to the policy of aggrandisement pursued by the emperors who, because they hoped ultimately to obtain for themselves the Pope's spiritual supremacy over the whole world, encouraged the Patriarchs in their disloyalty.—The schism was begun in the year 867, by Photius, the erudite, but unprincipled, Patriarch of Constantinople. Aided by his partisans, he held a council presided over by the Emperor at which sentence of deposition and excommunication was pronounced against the Pope, St. Nicholas I. The schism was healed, but began again in 1054 under the Patriarchate of Michael Cerularius and continues to the present day.— Between the fourth and the tenth century, Constantinople developed a peculiar rite, known as the Byzantine, and adopted Greek as the liturgical language. In the ninth century, SS. Cyril and Methodius converted the Bulgarians and Moravians, used the same rite, but translated the liturgy into Slavonic. From Bulgaria the Byzantine-Slavonic rite spread into Serbia and Russia.—Many

---

[8] 2 Pet. iii. 16.

of the Schismatic Greeks have returned to their allegiance, and are allowed by Rome to retain their rite and their particular liturgical language.—Since the break with Rome, the Schismatic Greeks speak of themselves as members of the "Orthodox Church," or "The True and Apostolic Church." Strictly speaking, the term "Schismatic *Greeks*" is inaccurate, since the majority of the Schismatics are not Greeks, but Slavs.

ITS DOCTRINES.—The Schismatic Greeks are one in faith with Catholics on almost all points, excepting the doctrines of the Immaculate Conception, and the Primacy and Infallibility of the Pope; they hold that the only infallible authority in the Church is a general council consisting of the bishops of the entire Church, Greek and Latin; hence, since they regard the Latin, or Catholic, Church as in error, and hold no communion with it, they maintain that, at the present time, no organ of infallibility exists, and they reject the decrees of all councils in which their bishops took no part; they hold that the Primacy of the Roman Pontiff is not of Divine, but of ecclesiastical, institution, and was transferred, at least, as regards the Greek, or Eastern Church, to the Patriarchate of Constantinople; the primacy of the Patriarch, however, they never interpreted as anything more than a primacy of honour. Still, it must not be thought that at the present time even this shadowy bond of reverence for the See of Constantinople exists. The Churches of Russia, Greece, and the Balkans—*i.e.*, about four-fifths of all the Schismatics—are completely separated from her and from one another.

**The Schismatic Greek Church is not the true Church.**—(1) The Schismatic Greek Church does not claim infallibility. Since its separation from Rome, it recognizes no living teaching-authority competent to decide infallibly matters of faith. (2) It claims Apostolicity, but unjustifiably as we shall show.[9] (3) It is not catholic either socially or numerically. Not socially, because it is confined chiefly to portions of the Greek and the Slavonic races. Nor numerically, because its total following is no more than 100 millions.[10]—But, even though it had a claim to catholicity, it has no claim to unity of government.[11] It is divided into fifteen churches, each claiming independence. It is really not a church but an assemblage of churches. In Greece, and the Balkans, it is

---

[9] See below, B. ii.   [10] See below, B. iii. footnote.

[11] Nor is it absolutely one in doctrine. Constantinople and Russia disagree as to the validity of Baptism conferred by a Protestant or Catholic. There are, also, several other points of difference which we need not detail.

little more than a state-department with the civil monarch as its highest official. In the Turkish dominions, by a most extraordinary anomaly, its bishops invoke the aid of the infidel government to settle their disputes. (4) The average level of sanctity among the laity of the Schismatic Greek Church is unquestionably high. This we may explain by the fact that it has preserved almost all the doctrines and devotions of the Catholic Church, that it has valid episcopal and priestly orders, and so still disposes of many of the means of grace. Yet, it must seem singular even to the Greeks themselves that, since they snapped the link with Rome, their Church appears to have remained in spiritual stagnation. It has had no saints, no martyrs, no miracles.—At any time in the future, there may be a re-awakening of intellectual life among its members, and its teaching authority may be questioned. Its faith, resting as it does on an insecure foundation, will not be proof against assault. Then will ensue either a return to Rome or the loss of all faith, followed ultimately by the loss of all sanctity.

The root-defect of the Schismatic Greek Church is its rejection of a supreme spiritual authority, the great unifying bond of the Church of Christ. At the time of their separation, the Greeks formed one body, united around the Patriarchate of Constantinople. Their unity, however, was not a unity of obedience, but of reverence, and has been riven to fragments by secular princes who require that each kingdom should have its own separate and subservient church.

§ 8.

**The Branch Theory.**—Since the Oxford Movement (1833-45) it has been a favourite theory with Anglican divines of the Ritualist party that the Church of Christ resembles a tree with three great branches, viz., the Church of England, the Greek Church, and the Catholic Church; the branches are distinct, yet they are of one tree, because each has Apostolic succession,[12] and all share in the same sacramental life; each is *the* Church of Christ in its own domain, so that men are bound on pain of schism to be members of it, not of another branch; the Church of England is for Englishmen, the Greek Church is for Greeks and Slavs, the Catholic Church is chiefly for the Latin races. This theory, they believe, reconciles the present divided state of the Church with the doctrine that she is one and continuous, but the difficulties against it are insuperable. In fact, it is mentioned here rather as a matter of historical interest than as having any serious place in religious controversy. It is ignored or rejected by the majority

---

[12] As to the Anglican claim to Apostolicity, see below B. ii.

of English Protestants, and is utterly repudiated by Greeks and Catholics. We are asked, then, to conceive a "branch" Church whose branches refuse to acknowledge its existence. Such a church would possess no unity of government: it would consist of mutually hostile bodies, each seeking the destruction of the other two, and would be utterly unlike the Church of St. Paul, the one living body of Christ, one in heart and mind. It would not be one in faith, for its creed would be a mass of ludicrous contradictions: its Catholic members would hold, while Greeks and Anglicans would reject, the Supremacy and Infallibility of the Pope, and the official Anglican Church[13] would regard as obligatory hardly any doctrine, professed in common by Greeks and Catholics. The analysis of the theory yields so many absurdities that it need not be continued further. We merely note in conclusion the following points:—(1) The assumption that the Anglican Church has a sacramental life, that its Bishops and Priests are validly ordained, with powers to consecrate and absolve, is rejected by a very large number, perhaps by the majority, of Anglicans themselves;—the Catholic Church has expressly decided against the validity of Anglican orders, and regards the Anglican Church, in point of sacramental power, as a broken cistern from which the waters of life have long disappeared. (2) The theory makes the extravagant supposition that faith varies with nationality, that Christ wished men to believe one thing because they were born in England, and quite the opposite because they were born in Italy.[14]

---

### B.—THE CATHOLIC CHURCH IS THE TRUE CHURCH.

Since the true Church is not the Protestant nor the Schismatic Greek Church, nor any combination of Protestants, Schismatic Greeks and Catholics, it must

---

[13] A member of the Anglican Church may hold, without imperilling his status, almost anything he pleases on the necessity and efficacy of Baptism, the Real Presence in the Eucharist, the sacramental nature of Matrimony, the Divine institution of the Episcopacy, the Resurrection of Our Lord and even His Divinity. Moreover he is bound to tolerate every doctrine which a court, appointed by the civil authority, may decide as tenable. It was this last consideration which finally decided the late Cardinal Manning to become a Catholic.

[14] It is unnecessary to consider whether the true Church may not consist of a combination of some two of the three Churches. The arguments against any such theory, if it were proposed, may be easily deduced from what has been already said.

be the Catholic Church.—Besides, the Catholic Church has all the marks of the true Church :—

I. **She claims Infallibility** (see Ch. IX.).—She claims that, since she speaks in the name of Christ, she is immune from error in defining the truth of which she is guardian and in condemning all doctrines contrary to it. When purity of doctrine is at stake, she is checked by no consideration of expediency. She prefers to lose whole nations rather than temporize in matters of faith.

II. **She claims Apostolicity** (see Ch. IX.).—The fact that she makes the claim is sufficient for our present purpose. For convenience sake, however, we discuss, without entering fully into proof or refutation, the arguments on which she and her rivals base their claims :—(1) The Bishops of the Church, she maintains, have succeeded to the authority of the Apostles. The Apostles formed a united body under the Primacy of St. Peter, and exercised their authority in submission to his. So, too, the Bishops form a united body under the Primacy of St. Peter's successor, the Pope. No Bishop can be a member of the Church or retain Apostolic authority, unless he be in communion with the head of the Church. Apostolicity, therefore, belongs to the Roman Catholic Church alone. Moreover, it is an historical fact, no longer disputed, that at the present day no See in the world but the See of Rome is linked in unbroken succession to an Apostle. Constantinople, called by courtesy Apostolic, was not founded by an Apostle. Antioch, St. Peter's first Bishopric, fell away from the Church in the Monophysite heresy[15] of the fifth century. A similar fate befell Alexandria, founded by St. Mark under the direction of St. Peter. Jerusalem, the See of St. James, had but a brief existence, perishing utterly at the destruction of the city

---

[15] The heresy of Eutyches, condemned at the General Council of Chalcedon (451). Eutyches taught that there are not two distinct natures in Christ; that His Humanity was absorbed in His Divinity.

by Titus in 70 A.D. There are no others. (2) The Schismatic Greeks, broken up as they are into independent churches, admit that, unlike us, Catholics, they have no central See communicating Apostolic authority to the rest, but they maintain that their doctrine is Apostolic. We reply that no church has any certainty that its doctrine is Apostolic, unless it can show that its authority to teach is derived from the Apostles. (3) Of the Protestant churches, the Anglican alone, or rather a section of it, claims Apostolicity. But, England was converted by emissaries from the Holy See. Her church retained Apostolicity, therefore, only so long as she remained in communion with Rome. Rome gave her Apostolicity, and Rome could, and did, deprive her of it.

III. **She is catholic or universal** (see Ch. IX.), **and at the same time, one in government, faith, and worship.**

(1) SHE IS CATHOLIC OR UNIVERSAL :—(a) She is catholic in desire, for she has at all times endeavoured to fulfil the command of Christ to teach all nations. Unlike the false sects whose missionary zeal is either non-existent or but a recent and feeble imitation of her own,[16] she has always felt that she had a duty to the heathen which she dared not neglect. Nor is she content with seeking fresh conquests among barbarous peoples, for she is constantly striving to regain the European territory she lost at the Reformation. Everywhere she chafes against her frontiers, and is insatiably eager to enlarge them.—(b) She is socially catholic, because, unlike the false sects, she is not confined wholly or chiefly to a single people; she

---

[16] The missionary efforts of the Schismatic Greeks are negligible. As to the Protestants, for nearly three centuries they completely ignored the command of Christ to teach all nations. Their foreign missions are practically confined to the British Empire, and, although supported by almost ten times the resources at the command of Catholics (£4,000,000 as against £480,000 per annum), are comparatively speaking a failure—a failure all the more remarkable in view of the fact that many of their missionaries are men of undoubted zeal.

belongs not to any nation, but to the world; she counts her members in every station of life, the poor and the illiterate as well as men eminent in every calling, statesmen, scientists, and writers. So powerful over the hearts and minds of men is the attraction of her doctrine and institutions that her adversaries are accustomed to speak of her as the sorceress of Rome, but her only spell is the spell of Christ to whose office of charity she has succeeded; she is to her followers what Christ was to the poor of Palestine, a light, a refuge, and a hope.—(c) She is numerically catholic. Her following numbers about 270 millions, and far exceeds that of any other Christian denomination.

(2) SHE IS NOT ONLY CATHOLIC, BUT ONE IN HER CATHOLICITY (see Ch. IX.)—ONE IN GOVERNMENT, FAITH, AND WORSHIP.—(a) *She is one in government* :—The people are subject to their priests, the priests and people to their Bishops, and all are subject to the Pope, the centre of authority, the bond of Apostolic unity. He commands their affection and their loyalty, not because of any personal considerations—he may be of the humblest origin, the counterpart of Peter the Fisherman, a man without pride of race or ancestry—but because, in their eyes, he is ennobled beyond any earthly potentate by the throne he fills; because, to them, he is the Elect of God, the Vicar of Christ. Nor are their relations to him adversely affected by any embitterment in their relations to one another. Divided by a real or fancied sense of wrong as to their material interests, they may be ranged on opposing sides in a terrible war. Still their allegiance to him will remain unimpaired. In the true spirit of their religion they will share the common hope that some day the frenzy of misunderstanding may cease, and that the nations of the world may bring their quarrels for adjustment to the Father of Christendom, the living representative of the Prince of Peace. (b) *She is one in faith.*—All her members, whether they be cultured Europeans

or children of the forest, hear the same doctrines from her priests or missionaries, and profess the same faith on penalty of exclusion from her fold. She bears the message of Christ and, courageous and plain-spoken as Himself, insists that it be received in its integrity. She shuts her ears to the sensual who look to her in vain for an abridgment of her moral teaching. She ignores the claims of false science and the demands of corrupt politicians. Men swayed by their passions or by the pride of intellect must bow down before the Divinely appointed teacher; they must accept with unquestioning assent the Trinity, the Incarnation,—all the profound mysteries of her creed; they must listen to the voice of Christ with the humility of children. Therein lies the miracle of her unity, that she, while teaching what is hard to believe, while prescribing what is hard to practise, while rejecting all compromise in faith or morals, yet holds her vast following together in willing submission. (c) *She is one in worship.*—Her sacraments and sacrifice are everywhere the same, and everywhere the faithful have access to the same ministrations; she tolerates differences of language and ceremonial, but nothing that affects essentials. She makes the highest as well as the lowest, the Cardinal as well as the peasant, the king as well as the cottier, kneel as humble penitents at the feet of her priests; and she brings them all to the altar to be fed with the Bread of Life. She is as absolute in regard to worship, as she is in regard to faith. As she suffers no diminution or alteration of her doctrine, so she will hear of no neglect of her sacraments. They are the means, given her by Christ for the sanctification of men; she sees that none of them be made void, but that each be applied as He intended. Her followers bear her yoke of worship as willingly as they bear her yoke of faith, thus exhibiting to the world the miraculous spectacle of a vast number of men, representing so many phases of human weakness, united, not for any material gain or sensual pleasure, but to participate in mysterious rites that may seem unreal, perhaps even repellent, to those who cannot see with the eyes of faith.

IV. **She is Holy** (see Ch. IX.).—She is holy, because she teaches, in addition to the other doctrines of Christ, His counsels of perfection, and succeeds in getting many of her children to practise them. She is in truth the mother of saints and martyrs. It is part of her very system to bless and encourage all who strive to attain to the higher Christian ideals, the ideals of charity, humility, and chastity. Hence, we see in her fold those great religious societies of men and women, who bind themselves by vows of poverty, chastity, and obedience, and who devote their lives to such practical works of charity as the education of youth, the relief of the poor, the support of orphans, the care of the sick and the aged, the rescue of the victims of sin; or, following the vocation for the contemplative life, spend their days in mortification and prayer. She is " the good tree " of the Gospel; she is the tree that, standing by the living waters, brings forth fruit in abundance. Christ Himself is with her and within her, and is multiplied in her children.—And she claims that Christ, in accordance with His promise, never ceases to attest her sanctity by miracles. We need not enter into a discussion of particular cases. It is sufficient to say that many of the miracles wrought in her communion cannot be disbelieved, unless we are prepared to reject everything founded on human testimony; further, that the very fact of her making such a claim is in itself an evidence of her truth.[16a]

**Conclusion:** The Catholic Church is, then, the only one that has all the marks of the true Church. Therefore, she must be the true Church.—Her claim to

---

[16a] On modern miracles, see Devas, *The Key to the World's Progress*, p. 80f, Longman's, Green, price 7d.

## THE IDENTIFICATION OF THE CHURCH OF CHRIST.

Infallibility would of itself alone be sufficient to prove that she is the true Church. The true Church must make that claim, and she alone makes it.—All the errors of the false sects may ultimately be reduced to a want of faith in the promise of Christ that He will always be with His Church. For, since Christ is always with her, she must be one with Him, one in heart and mind, *i.e.*, she cannot be divided either in obedience or in faith, she cannot tolerate either schism or heresy. That perfect unity is at once a proof of her truth and of the Divinity of her Founder, for He said at the Last Supper: " Not for them (*i.e.*, the Apostles) only do I pray, but for them also who through their word shall believe in Me; that they all may be one, as Thou, Father, in Me and I in Thee; that they also may be one in Us; that *the world may believe that Thou hast sent Me.*"[17]

**Objection** (1). The Church claims that, in virtue of her gift of Infallibility, her teaching never varies, that the faith of her children is always the same. This cannot be true, because from time to time she enlarges her creed by new definitions. Since the definition of the doctrine of the Immaculate Conception in 1854 all Catholics are bound to believe it. Before the definition they were free to reject it.

REPLY. The Church, by her definitions, does not enlarge her creed in the sense that she adds to it new articles of faith not found in the revelation of Christ to the Apostles. Her definitions are nothing more than fuller and more precise explanations of doctrines contained in the Deposit of Faith. The doctrine of the Immaculate Conception, for instance, is but a part of the doctrine always held by the Church that Mary is the Mother of the Redeemer, full of grace and sanctity, and that she loosed the knot of sin which Eve had fastened on the human race. The Church has not set forth the explicit and exhaustive meaning of all the profound truths entrusted to her. It is only as controversy, or some new devotion, arises that she decides whether a particular doctrine is, or is not, implicitly contained in those truths. The false sects, on the other hand, have no living voice, speaking with Divine authority, to determine doctrinal questions, hence interminable divisions, and the growth of new sects.—A new definition

[17] St. John xvii. 20, 21.

certainly creates a new obligation. But, the new obligation cannot press as a burden on the mass of the faithful who, in virtue of Passive Infallibility, have always believed all the doctrines explicitly or implicitly contained in the Deposit of Faith. It can affect but the very few who, as a fact, have not been one in faith with the Church. And even these, loyal Catholics as we assume them to be (for of others there is no question), will gladly relinquish an unwitting error, and will acquiesce at once and without demur in the infallible decision.

**Objection** (2). The Church has not always been one in government. During the Great Western Schism (1378-1417), the allegiance of the faithful was divided between two, and even three Popes.

Reply. Catholics were divided on a question of *identification*, not of *principle*. All acknowledged that there could be but one lawful Pope in the Church, but, owing to political disturbances and difficulties of communication, they were unable to identify him among the rival claimants. Some one of these was the lawful Pope, possessing Apostolic succession and authority. The Schism, although it was the source of many evils, proves God's solicitude for the preservation of the Papacy. For no human dynasty could have survived such a trial.[18]

---

## C.—PROOF OF THE TRUTH OF THE CATHOLIC CHURCH FROM HER MIRACULOUS STABILITY.

The stability of the Catholic Church is the marvel of her adversaries. It is only the hand of God that could have brought her safe through perils which have proved fatal to merely human institutions. Often she seemed rent with schism or corrupted by heresy. The pallor of death seemed to have come upon her, but, sustained by her Divine vitality, she cast off disease as a garment, and rose from her bed of sickness, renewed in youth and Pentecostal zeal. She is like the house of which Christ speaks in the Gospel : '' and the rain fell and the floods came, and they beat upon that house, and it fell not, for

---

[18] See following argument, end.

it was founded on a rock."[19] Often have her children heard the demons' exultant cry that, at last, she was whelmed in the wave of death. But the tempest passed, and day broke anew, and the eyes of men beheld her still firmly fixed as of old on the rock of Peter, triumphant amid the wreckage of her enemies.

"There is not," says the Protestant writer, Macaulay,[20] "and there never was on this earth, a work of human policy so well deserving of examination as the Roman Catholic Church. The history of that Church joins together the two great ages of human civilization . . . . The proudest royal houses are but of yesterday, when compared with the line of the Supreme Pontiffs. That line we trace back in unbroken series from the Pope who crowned Napoleon in the nineteenth century to the Pope who crowned Pepin in the eighth; and far beyond the time of Pepin the august dynasty extends. . . . . The republic of Venice came next in antiquity. But the republic of Venice was modern when compared with the Papacy; and the republic of Venice is gone, and the Papacy remains. The Papacy remains, not in decay, not a mere antique, but full of life and youthful vigour. The Catholic Church is still sending forth to the farthest ends of the world missionaries as zealous as those who landed in Kent with Augustine, and still confronting hostile kings with the same spirit with which she confronted Attila. . . . . Nor do we see any sign which indicates that the term of her long dominion is approaching. She saw the commencement of all the ecclesiastical establishments that now exist in the world; and we feel no assurance that she is not destined to see the end of them all. . . . . It is not strange that, in the year 1799, even sagacious observers should have thought that, at length, the hour of the Church of Rome was come. An infidel power ascendant, the Pope dying in captivity, the most illustrious prelates of France living in a foreign country

---

[15] St. Matt. vii 25.   [20] Essay on Ranke's *History of the Popes.*

on Protestant alms, the noblest edifices which the munificence of former ages had consecrated to the worship of God turned into temples of Victory, or into banqueting houses for political societies. . . . But the end was not yet. . . . Anarchy had had its day. A new order of things rose out of the confusion, new dynasties, new laws, new titles; and amidst them emerged the ancient religion. The Arabs have a fable that the Great Pyramid was built by antediluvian kings, and alone, of all the works of men, bore the weight of the flood. Such as this was the fate of the Papacy. It had been buried under the great inundation; but its deep foundations had remained unshaken; and, when the waters abated, it appeared alone amidst the ruins of a world that had passed away. The republic of Holland was gone, and the empire of Germany, and the great Council of Venice, and the old Helvetian League, and the House of Bourbon, and the parliaments and aristocracy of France. Europe was full of young creations, a French empire, a kingdom of Italy, a Confederation of the Rhine. Nor had the late events affected only territorial limits and political institutions. The distribution of property, the composition and spirit of society, had, through a great part of Catholic Europe, undergone a complete change. But the unchangeable Church was still there.''

The dangers to the Papacy came from within as well as from without. An elective monarchy, notoriously the most unstable of all forms of government, it attracted the ambition of worldly ecclesiastics and, for a time during the Middle Ages, became a prize for which rival monarchs intrigued, each trying to secure it for his own minion. It was, therefore, threatened with the twofold evil of an unworthy occupant and a disappointed faction. Hence, we find, as a fact, that there have been some few Popes, incompetent and even wicked, and that disastrous schisms have occurred from time to time. Any one of these schisms, any one of these Popes. if he had held a secular throne and were equally unfit for his office, would have brought the most powerful dynasty crashing to the ground. Moreover, the Papacy was threatened with another and, perhaps, greater, because more constant, danger, viz., the danger arising from ordinary human infirmity, for the Pope, when not exercising his gift of Infallibility, is liable to the errors of common men: St. Peter was upbraided to the face by St. Paul for his mistaken indulgence to the prejudices of Jewish converts, and some of his successors, though acting like him with the best intentions, seemed to bring the Church to the very brink of peril by their imprudence. We may, indeed, make no difficulty in admitting that, in the long history of the Papacy, there have been errors of policy which would have cost a temporal monarch his throne. It seems as though God wished to make of the occasional weakness of the Papacy a motive of credibility, a proof that the Church is Divinely supported. "The foolish things of the world hath God chosen," says St. Paul, " that he may confound the wise; and the weak things of the world hath God chosen that He may confound the strong. And the base things of the world, and the things that are contemptible hath God chosen, and things that are not, that He might bring to nought things that are: that no flesh should glory in His sight,"[21] *i.e.*, so that no man could take credit to himself for what had been the work of God. Again, we read in the Book of Judges how the Lord said to Gedeon: " The people that are with thee are many, and Madian shall not be delivered into their hands, lest Israel should glory against Me, and say: I was delivered by my own strength." So He bade him keep but 300 men of the assembled host of 32,000. Gedeon obeyed, and with this insignificant force he put a great army to rout. And as the hand of God was manifest in the triumph of Gedeon in spite of

---

[21] 1 Cor, i. 27, 29.

inferiority of numbers, so has it been manifest in the survival of the Papacy in spite of the occasional weakness or unworthiness of those who have sat on the throne of Peter.

We may summarize the argument as follows:—(1) The Papacy, the foundation on which the Church is built, is the only institution which has survived all the vast social and political changes and revolutions in the life and government of Europe since the days of the Roman Emperors. (2) It has survived in spite of persecution, and political intrigue; in spite of heresy and schism among its subjects; in spite of the worldliness and the weakness or incompetency of some of the Popes. (3) It has survived, not as a mere shadow of its former greatness, but in unimpaired vigour.—Such a survival is miraculous. The Papacy and the Church over which it presides must, therefore, be the work of God.

When Gladstone, angered by the decree of the Vatican Council and by the publication of a list of propositions condemned by the Holy See, asked contemptuously whether Rome could hope " to refurbish her rusty tools " and harness the avenging power of God to her excommunications in the modern world, he was reminded by Newman that the Pope who, in the Middle Ages, made Henry, the German Emperor, do penance bare-foot in the snow at Canossa, had had his counterpart in that other Pope who, in the nineteenth century, and by an actual interposition of Providence, inflicted a " snow-penance " on the Emperor Napoleon. We quote the memorable words of the Protestant historian, Alison[22]:—
" ' What does the Pope mean,' said Napoleon to Eugene, in July, 1807, ' by the threat of excommunicating me? Does he think the world has gone back a thousand years? Does he suppose the arms will fall from the hands of my soldiers '? Within two years after these remarkable words were written, the Pope did excommunicate him, in return for the confiscation of his whole dominions, and in less than four years more, the arms did fall from the hands of his soldiers; and the hosts, apparently invincible, which he had collected, were dispersed and ruined by the blasts of winter. ' The weapons of the soldiers,' says Segur, in describing the Russian retreat, ' appeared of an insupportable weight to their stiffened

---

[22] History, ch. 60.

arms. During their frequent falls they fell from their hands, and, destitute of the power of raising them from the ground, they were left in the snow. They did not throw them away: famine and cold tore them from their grasp.'" And Alison adds: "There is something in these marvellous coincidences beyond the operations of chance, and which even a Protestant historian feels himself bound to mark for the observation of future ages. The world had not gone back a thousand years, but that Being existed with whom a thousand years are as one day, and one day as a thousand years."[23] And as He was with Pope Gregory in 1077, so He was with Pope Pius in 1812, and so shall He be with some future Pope again, when the need shall come, and show to His enemies that His arm has not forgotten its strength.

[Read *Bishop Gore and the Catholic Claims*, by Dom Chapman, O.S.B., Longmans, Green, price 7d.

## III.

### NON-CHRISTIAN RELIGIONS.

Christ, the Son of God, founded His Church to teach His religion to all men. Therefore, all non-Christian religions must be rejected as false.

*Buddhism.*—Buddhism is an offshoot of pantheistic Brahminism, the ancient religion of India. Its founder was Siddhartha of the family Gautama. He was also called Sakya-muni (from *Sakya*, the name of his tribe, and *muni*, a solitary), but he is more commonly known by his sacred title, The Buddha, *i.e.*, "the enlightened." The son of a petty king, he was born at Kapilavastu in the north of India, towards the close of the sixth century B.C. (1) He adopted the Brahministic doctrine of the transmigration of souls; he held (2) that there is a supreme physical law of retribution in virtue of which good is rewarded and evil punished; (3) that existence is evil, because it brings with it old age, sickness, and death; (4) that souls come to re-birth, if in a previous state they were not free from desire, or from attachment to existence; (5) that a being attains perfection only when desire ceases, for it is only then that it can be admitted into the Nirvana, a state which cannot be exactly described, but which is apparently either annihilation, eternal sleep, or the absorption of personality. He did not deny that gods exist, but affirmed that, in as much as they exist, they are evil, and like other existing things can attain to perfection only in the Nirvana. The impersonal force, manifesting itself in the law of retribution, or in the

---

[23] Quoted by Newman, *Difficulties of Anglicans*, vol. ii., pp. 215. 216.

whole system of laws governing the conditions of all being, may, perhaps, represent Buddha's concept of a supreme God. His ethical teaching is, briefly, that man must suppress his passions and desires, and practise absolute self-denial, if he wishes to hasten his entrance into the Nirvana. The motive of virtue is, therefore, self-interest. Buddhism spread rapidly through India, Ceylon, Burmah, Tibet, China, and Japan. We may account for its propagation (1) by the obscurity of the older religion which it supplanted, but chiefly (2) by the fragments of truth found even in its central doctrine; (3) by its implicit denial of the existence of a Personal God, the Lawgiver Who will reward the good and punish the wicked; (4) by its toleration of sin, for it taught that those who indulged their passions did not lose, but merely delayed, their final happiness. In these last two respects, as well as in its doctrine of the motive of virtue, it differed widely from Christianity. Its adherents are said to number over four hundred millions. This, however, is quite inaccurate. Under the name of Buddhism are included very many sects with irreconcilable doctrines. Probably, pure Buddhism is now professed by considerably less than 100 millions. In any case, it has no claim to be considered a universal religion. It is restricted to Eastern peoples. Many of its doctrines are mere absurdities, or mere gratuitous assertions without any reasonable basis, and could not possibly receive any countenance except among men of a low grade of civilization.

*Mohammedanism.*—The religion of Islam (*i.e.*, "submission to God's decrees"), as it is called by its followers, was founded by Mohammed. He was born at Mecca in Arabia, 570 A.D. In early life he was a shepherd, but later became a merchant, and travelled to Syria and Palestine. He was much given to prayer and fasting, and was subject to epileptic fits. In his fortieth year he professed to have received a call from the Angel Gabriel to preach the worship of the one, true God to his people, the Arabs, who, though descended from Heber and Abraham, had lost the purity of their primitive belief, and had fallen into idolatry. His preaching was rejected at Mecca. He fled to Medina, where he succeeded in making many converts and in organizing a small army. In spite of some severe reverses, he was enabled by his talents as a general and leader to crush in detail the warring factions of Arabia, and to weld them into a formidable military state (630 A.D.). Towards the close of his life he showed himself a monster of lust, cruelty, and rapacity. He died in 633 A.D.—The sum of his doctrinal teaching is expressed in the formula: "There is no God but the true God, and Mohammed is His prophet." This single confession, however, implies six articles, viz., belief in (*a*) the unity of God; (b) His angels; (c) His scripture—Al Koran, the sacred book which Mohammed wrote; (d) His prophets—among whom are reckoned Adam, Noah, Abraham, Moses, Christ, and Mohammed himself, the last and greatest of all; (e) the Resurrection and Day of Judgment; (f) God's absolute and irrevocable decree, predetermining all things, good and evil (Fatalism). His moral teaching is concerned almost entirely with externals. It includes forms of prayer, alms, fasting, the obligation of making a pilgrimage to Mecca, and of waging war against the infidel. It permits polygamy and divorce, and approves of slavery. The motive to virtue is the assurance of admission after death to a paradise of fantastic sensuality.—Within a hundred years after Mohammed's death, a succession of able generals spread his religion through all the neighbouring countries, along the North African coast, into Spain, and even across the Pyrenees. But the tide of conquest was stemmed at Tours by Charles Martel, 732.— Its rapid propagation was due (1), as in the case of Buddhism, to the clearness and consistency of its monotheistic doctrine in contrast with the confused and contradictory teaching of polytheism; (2) to its pandering to base passions; but above all (3) to the might of the sword. At the present day, it has about 223 million followers, nine-tenths of whom belong to the Sunnite or Orthodox sect, under the headship of the Sultan of Turkey. It is said that there are, in all, 73 sub-divisions of Mohammedans, but it must be admitted that in the essentials of doctrine and practice they hardly differ.—The fragments of revealed truth which the religion contains were borrowed from Judaism or Christianity. Its fatalism, its low morality, its gross conception of eternal happiness, and the character of its founder stamp it plainly with falsehood, and make its propagation impossible among civilized peoples. It is professed chiefly by undeveloped or unprogressive races, it clings to the old lines of Mohammedan conquest, and owes almost all its present strength to political support.

# CHAPTER XI.

## THE GOVERNMENT OF THE CHURCH OF CHRIST.

### THE PAPACY.

*Summary.*

I. The Primacy of the Pope :—
   A. The doctrine of the Primacy, defined by the Church.
   B. The arguments from Scripture :—
      (*a*) the Primacy promised to St. Peter : " Thou art Peter, etc."
      (*b*) The Primacy conferred on St. Peter : " Feed my lambs, etc."
   C. Historical evidence for the Primacy (Tradition).

II. The Infallibility of the Pope :—
   A. The doctrine of Papal Infallibility, defined by the Church.
   B. The arguments from Scripture :—Texts as above with St. Luke xxi. 31, 32.
   C. An argument from reason.
   D. Historical evidence for Papal Infallibility (Tradition).

III. Some misconceptions removed—The Pope's ordinary teaching, distinguished from his infallible teaching — Objections answered :—Galileo, Liberius, Honorius, the Inquisition—Outside the Church there is no salvation—The Church and the State.

   Appendix : Christ, a living force : an argument for His Divinity.

**Note:** *Since the Catholic Church is the true Church of Christ, since she speaks in His name and is infallible, the fact that she teaches a doctrine must be regarded as in itself decisive of its truth, quite independently of any arguments in its favour from the S. Scriptures or other sources.*

# THE GOVERNMENT OF THE CHURCH OF CHRIST.

## I.

### THE PRIMACY OF THE POPE.

**A. The Teaching of the Church.**—The Vatican Council (1870) has defined: (1) that St. Peter was appointed by Christ visible Head of the Church; (2) that he received from Christ a Primacy, not only of honour, but of jurisdiction, *i.e.*, that he received from Christ supreme authority to teach and govern the whole Church; (3) that he has, in virtue of the same Divine institution, a perpetual line of successors in the Primacy; (4) that his successors are the Roman Pontiffs.—Christ Himself is the invisible Head of the Church. From Him all power in the Church is derived. He will remain with it for ever, guiding, governing, and supporting it.

**B. Arguments from S. Scripture for the Primacy.**

(*a*) THE PRIMACY PROMISED TO ST. PETER.—Christ said to His disciples: " Whom do you say that I am?" Simon Peter answered and said : " Thou art Christ, the Son of the living God." And Jesus . . said to him: " Blessed art thou, Simon Bar-Jona . . . And I say to thee : Thou art Peter " (*i.e.*, the Rock) " and upon this rock I will build My Church, and the gates of hell shall not prevail against it. And I will give to thee the keys of the kingdom of heaven. And whatsoever thou shalt bind upon earth, it shall be bound also in heaven; and whatsoever thou shalt loose on earth, it shall be loosed also in heaven."[1] The text must be interpreted as follows :—

(1) Christ compares His Church to a house which shall be built on a rock. As the rock gives stability to the house,[2] so shall St. Peter give stability to the Church:

---

[1] St. Matt. xvi. 15-19.
[2] St. Matt. vii. 25, " the house fell not, for it was founded on a rock."

he shall make the Church so firm that the gates of hell —*i.e.*, death, the power of its enemies—shall never destroy it. But, since Christ promises that St. Peter, being the rock, shall alone make the Church proof against all assaults, it follows that St. Peter is to be the source of all its stability, that he is to be at once the foundation and the support of the Divine edifice. The sustaining strength of St. Peter, therefore, shall be felt in every part of the Church and by every member of it without exception. In a society it is the Supreme Authority which gives stability, hence St. Peter's office in the Church shall be that of Supreme Authority. He shall shield the Church from the great evil of heresy : he shall, therefore, be the teacher of the entire Church, and shall never teach any doctrine but the true doctrine of Christ. He shall shield the Church from the great evil of schism : he shall be the ruler of the entire Church, never tolerating a rival authority, never allowing the Church to break up into independent sections. He shall cast out the heretical and the rebellious, and hold the faithful firmly together, one in faith and obedience.

(2) The promise of the Primacy is directly stated in the words : " and I will give to thee the keys of the Kingdom of Heaven," *i.e.*, the keys of the Church. The keys were regarded by the Jews, as they are regarded by us, as a symbol of ownership or supreme authority. He who holds the keys is master of the house. St. Peter, therefore, shall be master or ruler of the Church.

(3) He shall receive the powers of " binding " and " loosing," *i.e.*, he shall have power to issue decrees; to make laws or annul them; to judge, condemn, or acquit; to grant or withhold absolution from sin. The same powers are, indeed, promised to all the Apostles in St. Matt xviii. 18, but from the fact that they were first promised to St. Peter, the rock and the holder of the keys, it is clear that his fellow-Apostles are to exercise them subordinately to his authority. We make a like com-

ment on the words of St. Paul that the Church is built "on the foundation of the Apostles."[3] It is built on them as forming a united body under the Primacy of St. Peter.

(*b*) THE PRIMACY CONFERRED ON ST. PETER AND HIS SUCCESSORS.—Christ promised the Primacy to St. Peter on hearing him make a profession of faith in His Divinity. He fulfils the promise on hearing him make a triple protestation of love for Him. "Feed my lambs," He said to Peter, "feed my sheep."[4] St. Peter thus was made shepherd of the whole flock of Christ. All the members of the Church, including his fellow-Apostles themselves, were placed under his supreme jurisdiction or authority. His office in the Church is perpetual: (1) "The 'lambs' and 'sheep,'" *i.e.*, the members of the Church, shall always need the shepherd's care to shield them from the wolf and to lead them to wholesome pastures; their shepherd, therefore, St. Peter, through his successors, shall be always with them. (2) The Church, and, with it, its foundation and support, is to last until the end of time; St. Peter, therefore, through his successors, shall be always with the Church, guarding its life, and giving it strength to withstand its enemies. He, through them, shall be the source of its imperishability.

C. **Historical Evidence for the Primacy**. (TRADITION).—(1) From the fifth century onward the Primacy of the Pope as the successor of St. Peter was universally admitted. At the Council of Ephesus (431), Philip, the Legate of Pope Celestine (422-432), said, and no voice was raised in protest: "No one doubts, nay but all ages know, that the holy and most blessed Peter, prince and head of the Apostles, the pillar of the faith and the foundation of the Church, received from Our Lord, Jesus Christ, the keys of the Kingdom. . . . His successor in

---

[3] Eph. ii. 20.       [4] St. John xxi. 15-17.

order, and the holder of his place, our holy and most blessed Pope, Celestine . . . has sent me," etc. St. Cyril of Alexandria (†444), pre-eminent among the Eastern Patriarchs, said that Pope Celestine was "the chief Bishop of the whole world."[5] At the Council of Chalcedon (451), when the letter of Pope Leo I. (440-461) had been read, the assembled bishops cried out: "Peter has spoken through Leo."—(2) In the fourth century,[6] the evidence, though less in volume, is equally decisive. "I speak," said St. Jerome to Pope Damasus (366-384), "with the successor of the fisherman. . . . I, following no one as my chief but Christ, am associated in communion with thy blessedness, that is, with the See of Peter. I know that on that rock the Church is built." St. Basil urges the same Pope to deal with troubles that had arisen in the Churches of Asia Minor; he adds that he requests nothing new, and quotes as a precedent for the Pope's intervention the action of his predecessor, Pope Dionysius (259-269).[7]—(3) In the earlier centuries the evidence is not so clear, (a) because the Church suffered much from persecution, and communication with the Pope was difficult; and (b) because the early Christians, being still in their first fervour, "of one heart and one soul," gave little occasion for the exercise of the Papal prerogative; there was a development in government as well as in matters of faith; opposition, as it arose from time to time, called forth a more explicit statement of doctrine, and a clearer enunciation of the relations of the Pope to the universal Church. Still, we note, even in the first century, the remarkable fact that Pope

---

[5] Migne, 77, 1040.

[6] Carvings and ornamentations in the catacombs dating from this century represent (1) St. Peter as the Moses of the New Testament receiving the New Law from Christ, and (2) Moses as the Peter of the Old Testament. Peter was the leader of the Christians, as Moses was the leader of the Jews.

[7] See Newman, *Development of Christian Doctrine*, ch iv. 3; vi. 3, where a much fuller list of authorities, with references, will be found.

Clement (91-100), while St. John the Apostle was still living, writes, as one commanding, to the Church of Corinth, condemns those who have disturbed its peace, and warns them against disobeying what Christ had said through him. (4) As to St. Peter himself, we find that, in the Gospels, his name is always mentioned first in the lists of the Apostles, although he was not the first whom Christ called; he proposes the election of the successor to Judas; he preaches the first Apostolic sermon on the Feast of Pentecost; he works the first Apostolic miracle in the name of Jesus; he receives the first Jewish converts and the first Gentile converts into the Church, declaring that salvation is for all men alike; at the Council of Jerusalem, " when there had been much disputing,"[7a] he gives the discussion a decisive turn, and draws the others with him—all this, though it may not by itself prove, yet seems to indicate, and is quite consistent with, a primacy of jurisdiction.—In fine, be it noted: (a) that the belief in the Primacy of the Pope, universal in the fifth century, and distinctly expressed in the fourth, if it be not as old as the Church, must have been fraudulently invented during the ages of persecution; in other words, either we must admit the Apostolic origin of the doctrine, or else maintain the gross absurdity that it was forged at a time when the chief office among Christians was the surest road to martyrdom; (b) that, since the Church is infallible, a doctrine universally taught and believed at any time as part of the faith of the Church must be true; and (c) that the Bishop of Rome must be the successor of St. Peter, for he alone of all the bishops in Christendom has ever claimed the title.

---

7a See *Acts* xv.

## II.

### THE INFALLIBILITY OF THE POPE.

**A. The Teaching of the Church.**—The doctrine defined by the Vatican Council may be briefly stated as follows:—The Pope is infallible when he speaks *ex cathedra*, *i.e.*, when, as Pastor and Teacher of all Christians, he defines, in virtue of his supreme Apostolical authority, a doctrine concerning faith or morals to be held by the Universal Church. He is said to "define" a doctrine, when he makes it clear that the doctrine must be believed with a firm, interior assent of faith. The doctrine must be concerned with faith or morals and must belong to the Deposit of Faith,[8] *i.e.*, it must be found in Scripture or Tradition.

**B. Arguments from S. Scripture for Papal Infallibility.**—(1) St. Peter, always living in his successors, is the rock on which the Church is built. He shall, through the assistance of Christ, always with him, save the Church from heresy.[9] He, the one and only source of stability, cannot be a false or doubtful guide. He must, therefore, be infallible. (2) Christ gave to St. Peter and his successors "the keys of the Kingdom of Heaven." He gave them thereby the power of binding the consciences of men. He promised that whatever obligations they might impose would be confirmed in heaven. In other

---

[8] It is certain that infallibility extends, also, to doctrines which, though no part of the Deposit of Faith, are intimately connected with it, and are necessary for its custody. See ch. ix. A end, p. 88.

[9] See above B (1).

words, He promised to support and guide them in teaching the truth so that they would never impose any but a just obligation. But the Head of the Church is the chief teacher of the Church, and does, as a fact, from time to time, bind all the faithful to believe his teaching and to believe it with an assent of faith. Since, from the promise of Christ, he cannot bind them to error, he must himself be secured against error in his teaching, he must be infallible.—(3) The Pope is the Pastor of the Universal Church. " Feed my lambs," said Christ to St. Peter, " feed my sheep." He has the command of Christ to feed all the faithful with spiritual nurture, to teach them the doctrines of Christ, to administer to them the sacred rites which Christ instituted, to govern them in the form, and under the laws, prescribed by Christ. But, if the Pope were to err in his *ex cathedra* teaching, he would not be the pastor, but the poisoner, of his flock. Therefore, he must be infallible.—(4) Christ said to St. Peter: " Simon, Simon, behold Satan hath desired to have *you*, that he may sift *you* as wheat. But I have prayed for *thee* that *thy* faith fail not: and do *thou* . . . confirm thy brethren."[10] Christ says He had prayed that St. Peter's faith should not fail. No one can doubt that His prayer, the prayer of the Son of God, to His heavenly Father, was heard. His very words clearly indicate it, for He said, in effect, " I have prayed for thee that thy faith fail not, and do thou *with that faith My prayer has won for thee* confirm thy brethren." St. Peter, therefore, was made infallible. He was to use his gift of infallibility to shield the faith of his brethren from the assaults of Satan.—His office passed to his successors: as long as the Church exists, it will be assailed by the enemy of truth; it will, therefore, always need an unerring guide, a Peter living in his successors who shall

---

[10] St. Luke xxi. 31, 32.

confirm his brethren.[11]—(5) Independently of the text, "Thou art Peter," etc., we proved that the Church is infallible.[12] But, in an infallible Church, the supreme judge of doctrine must be infallible. The Pope is the supreme judge of doctrine, because, since he is the supreme ruler, his decision on all questions affecting the teaching, the governing, or the sanctifying office of the Church, must be final.

C. **Argument from Reason for Papal Infallibility.**—Reason itself demands that there should be in the Church an organ of infallibility capable of dealing with manifest corruptions of doctrine at their very inception. Such an organ of infallibility is found in the supreme teaching authority of the Pope. His prompt decision will spare the Church a multitude of evils. The only other organ of infallibility of which there can be any question is a General Council, *i.e.*, a council consisting of a large number of bishops, representative of the entire Church, assembled at the summons or with the approval of the Pope, and passing doctrinal or disciplinary decrees which he confirms. Such a large body, it is manifest, cannot be assembled without long delay, and, at times, owing to wars or other disturbances, cannot be assembled at all.

D. **Historical Evidence for Papal Infallibility.** (TRADITION).—The voice of tradition, as in the case of the Primacy, grows clearer with the progress of the cen-

---

[11] Arguing from the doctrine, held by Protestants as well as Catholics, that each of the Apostles was infallible, we conclude that Christ's words do not refer to them as individuals, for they did not need St. Peter's help to preserve them from error. Christ, therefore, spoke of them in their representative capacity. He meant that St. Peter alone would transmit his infallibility to his successors, that he, through them, was to confirm in faith the Bishops, the successors of the other Apostles. The Protestant teaching that St. Peter's infallibility, like that of the other Apostles, was a personal prerogative, and, therefore, intransmissible, is irreconcilable with any reasonable interpretation of the text.

[12] See ch. ix. p. 87

turies. (1) Towards the end of the second century, St. Irenaeus praises the See of Rome as "the greatest Church," and says that the faithful everywhere "must resort to it" or "must agree with it."[13] (2) About the beginning of the third century, Pope Zephyrinus condemns the Montanists,[13a] who thenceforward are regarded as outcasts from the Church. (3) In the fourth century, Pope St. Julius remonstrated (342) with the Eusebians: "Why were we not written to concerning the Church of Alexandria? or, are you ignorant that this has been the custom first to write to us, and then what is just to be decreed from this place. . . . For what we have received from the blessed Apostle Peter, that I make known to you."[14] (4) In the fifth century, the bishops at the Council of Chalcedon (451) in the words already quoted said, "Peter has spoken through Leo." They subscribed to his definition of faith, saying "This is the faith of the Fathers; we all follow it."[15]—From this century onward the doctrine was universally acknowledged in the practical life of the Church. It was accepted at the third Council of Constantinople (680-681), and all but defined in express terms by the Council of Florence (1438-1445), which declared "that the Roman Pontiff is the successor of St. Peter, . . . and the true Vicar of Christ, the head of the whole Church, the father and teacher of all Christians, and that to him, in Blessed Peter, Our Lord Jesus Christ gave full power to feed, to rule, and to govern the entire Church."

### III.

**Misconceptions as to Papal Infallibility.**—To remove some gross misconceptions—Papal Infallibility does not imply impeccability, or sinlessness. The Pope is infallible in doctrine, but not

---

[13] Adv. Haer. III. 3.—In either interpretation the words refer to a higher doctrinal authority. [13a] Their founder, Montanus, claimed to be a prophet sent by God to supplement the moral teaching of Christ. [14] Athanasius, *Apologia contra Arianos*, n. 33. [15] Hardiun, t. 2, p 656.—See Newman, *op. cit.* for fuller list of authorities.

impeccable in conduct. He must work out his salvation " in fear and trembling " like other men, sharing with St. Paul the apprehension " lest, perhaps, when I have preached to others, I myself should become a castaway."[16] Neither does Papal Infallibility imply a power to make new revelations, *i.e.*, to disclose to man Divine truths previously unknown. The whole Christian revelation was delivered to the Apostles. The Pope, in the exercise of Infallibility, merely explains it without adding anything to it. Nor are his infallible utterances inspired. For inspiration we require:—(*a*) that the writer or speaker be moved by God Himself to write or speak; and (*b*) that he be so guided by God, while writing or speaking, that he expresses what God Himself wishes to express and nothing more. God is the author of inspired utterances. He is not the author of Papal definitions, but He guarantees them against error.

**Twofold Teaching Authority of the Pope.**—The Pope possesses a twofold teaching authority, viz., supreme or infallible and ordinary.[17] When he employs his ordinary authority, he is not infallible and does not, of course, bind us to an assent of faith. Still, it is the common and safe opinion that we must give his teaching an interior, religious assent. The obligation arises (1) from the obedience which we owe, as dutiful children, to lawful ecclesiastical authority, and (2) from prudence, which forbids us to set our opinion against the great authority of the Pope, familiar, as he must be, with the traditions of the Church, and aided, as he is, by the counsel of eminent theologians. Should it happen—in the nature of things, it must happen very rarely—that learned Catholics see, or think they see, grave reasons for doubting some point in the ordinary teaching of his Holiness, they may represent their views to him, but must do so privately, respectfully, and with a profession of complete willingness to accept his final ruling in the proper spirit of obedience.

**Objections against Papal Infallibility.**—Protestants mention four Popes as having erred, viz., Paul V. and Urban VIII., who condemned Galileo; Liberius and Honorius, who are said to have fallen into heresy, the former into Arianism, the latter into Monothelism. Our general reply is that the conditions required for an infallible decision were not present in any of these cases:

---

[16] 1 Cor. ix. 27.

[17] The Pope teaches the Church with his ordinary authority either directly, or through one of the Roman Congregations, *i.e.*, through one of the committees of learned men who assist him in his work. The Congregation of the Holy Office or Inquisition and the Congregation of the Index are concerned with purity of doctrine; the Biblical Commission, with questions connected with the S. Scriptures.

## THE GOVERNMENT OF THE CHURCH OF CHRIST.

(1) *Paul V., Urban VIII. and Galileo.*—Paul V. in 1616 and Urban VIII. in 1633, acting through the Congregations of the Holy Office and the Index, condemned as heretical the teaching of Galileo (1564-1642) that the sun is immovable, and that the earth rotates daily on its axis. The astronomer would most certainly have escaped all censure but for his imprudence in applying his doctrine to the interpretation of the passage in the Book of Josue (x. 13) where it is said that the sun stood still. He undoubtedly suffered for his opinions in the sense that, for many years, he had to endure much mental distress. As for physical punishment, he was not " tortured " nor " cast into a dungeon," as our enemies used to say, but was kept for a short time in honourable confinement. Copernicus (1473-1543) and Cardinal Nicholas of Cusa, his predecessors in astronomical research, had advocated the same opinions without molestation. His condemnation does not affect the doctrine of the Infallibility of the Pope, for the Popes in question did not teach *ex cathedra*. A Pope cannot delegate his infallibility to a Congregation. He must, himself, personally address the Universal Church, and require that his teaching be accepted by all its members with the assent of faith. This condition was not verified in the case of Paul and Urban.—That there was no question of an irreversible decision is perfectly clear from the words of Cardinal Bellarmine (1542-1641), a member of the Congregation of the Holy Office which condemned Galileo. Writing to Galileo's friend, Foscarini, he says that there would be no objection to putting forward the new system as the best explanation of celestial phenomena, provided no reference were made to the apparent conflict with the Bible. And he continues : " I say that if a real proof be found that the sun is fixed, and does not revolve round the earth, but the earth round the sun, then it will be necessary very carefully to proceed to the explanation of the passages of Scripture which appear to be contrary, as we should prefer to say that we have misunderstood these rather than pronounce that to be false which is demonstrated."

But, though the condemnation of Galileo proves nothing against the Infallibility of the Pope, may it not be said that it proves the hostility of the Church to scientific progress and freedom of research? In reply, we put forward the following considerations :—
(1) Since the great majority of contemporary physicists and astronomers treated Galileo's opinions with derision,[18] the most

---

[18] Some of Galileo's arguments were undoubtedly worthless, and have since been abandoned. Professor Huxley, an unexpected witness, declares that " the Pope and Cardinals had rather the best of it," *Life and Letters*, ii, 424.—Of Galileo's contemporaries, Bacon, the so-called coryphæus of modern methods, was as hostile to him as any.

that can reasonably be urged against the Church in not immediately adopting them is that she was not in advance of her age. (2) No Protestant can complain of the Church's treatment of Galileo in view of the attitude of the Reformers to Copernicus some generations earlier. Luther denounced him as an arrogant fool who sought to overthrow all scientific astronomy and who contradicted Holy Writ. Melanchthon wished his pestilent doctrines to be suppressed by the civil power. (3) When physical science appears to demand a new interpretation of some statement in the Scriptures bearing on natural phenomena or such like, the attitude of the Church, as any impartial non-Catholic would admit, must be conservative; her procedure will be exactly as Cardinal Bellarmine describes it (see quotation above); she will disregard the unsupported word of one or two scientists; she will move only when she is assured that unanimity of scientific teaching demands a revision of the traditional interpretation. (4) The Church may, by her slowness to accept what is new, cause a temporary retardation of progress, but she rightly regards the custody of faith as something immeasurably more precious than the interests of physical science. And, for her, the custody of faith is bound up with the custody of tradition. Hence, even though no point of faith be at issue, she will not depart from tradition, until it is made perfectly clear to her that in the particular instance tradition is at fault.

It may be asked why does not the Pope pronounce at once infallibly on all questions submitted to him. The answer is that, although it is within his power to deliver, when he pleases, an infallible decision, still he holds himself bound to refrain from exercising his infallibility, until he has first done all that human industry can do, by study and careful inquiry, to ascertain the mind of the Church.[19] It follows, therefore, that his infallible decisions, except in cases of manifestly corrupt doctrine,[20] must be of rare occurrence, and that, in dealing with the numerous questions submitted to him, he must, as a rule, employ his ordinary or non-infallible teaching authority.

*Pope Liberius* (351-366).—Liberius on refusing to confirm an Arian[21] formulary of faith was exiled (355) by the Emperor Constantine. Two years later he was permitted to return to Rome. Some say, while others, and very weighty authorities, deny, that he purchased his liberty by acceding to the Emperor's wishes.

---

[19] God does not wish His human instruments to be merely passive. He wishes them to be active, to think and reason. Hence, even inspiration does not exclude industry and research.
[20] See II. C. above.
[21] The Arians denied the Divinity of Christ.

Let us suppose that he did sign the formulary:—(1) It cannot be shown that it contained anything erroneous: many of the Arian formularies were unobjectionable; (2) he did not sign as teacher of the Universal Church; he signed as a prisoner and under compulsion; manifestly it cannot be held that, in such circumstances he intended to bind the consciences of the faithful.

*Pope Honorius* (625-638).—Honorius wrote two letters, one to Sergius, an advocate of the Monothelite[22] heresy, another to Sophronius, the champion of orthodoxy, in which he forbade further discussion and declared that "there is but one Will in Christ." Honorius was anathematized as a heretic by the General Council of Constantinople (680-1). His case, however, yields no argument against Papal Infallibility:—(1) Honorius did not pronounce a definition *ex cathedra*, for, he said expressly, " It doth not behove us to settle the question whether the number of operations in Christ is one or two "; he had been misinformed by Sergius as to the point at issue, and thought that the controversy was, as he observed, " a war of words " to be settled by " grammarians." (2) His words bear an orthodox sense; they were written to contradict the false doctrine, ascribed by Sergius to his opponent, " that there are two *conflicting* Wills in Christ." (3) The decree of the Council of Constantinople must be regarded as condemnatory of the conduct of Honorius, not of his teaching as Head of the Church. So much is clear from the words of Pope Leo II., who explained that he had confirmed the decree, because Honorius had been negligent " in extinguishing the rising flame of heresy." The decree of a General Council is infallible only in the sense in which it is ratified by the Pope. It is, however, much disputed whether the Fathers of Constantinople intended to stigmatize Honorius as a heretic in the modern acceptation of the term. The word seems to have been applied in those days to anyone whose action, apart from any positive teaching, was thought to favour heresy or schism.

**The Ecclesiastical and the Spanish Inquisition.**—*The Ecclesiastical Inquisition.*—During the twelfth and thirteenth centuries, violent sectaries made their appearance in several parts of southern Europe. They attacked the clergy, destroyed churches and monasteries, and encouraged revolt against civil authority. The whole fabric of society, political and religious, was threatened with disruption. To meet so grave a peril, the Church, in concert with the secular governments, established (1231) the Roman or Eccle-

---

[22] The monothelites taught that there was no distinct Human Will in Christ; that it was absorbed in the Divine. In other words, they taught that Christ was not true man.

siastical Inquisition to try charges of heresy. Its tribunals were set up in several countries, as need arose. Its object was primarily corrective. If the heretic were prepared to recant his errors, it imposed a penance on him, sometimes very light, and reconciled him with the Church; if he were obdurate, it pronounced him guilty of heresy, and handed him over to the State for punishment. The State passed sentence, and its judgments were severe—confiscation of property, imprisonment, or death itself. Officially, the Church never condemned anyone to death, but she undoubtedly approved of the stern repression of heresy by the State, and believed that, in the circumstances of the age, she was justified in her approval.—The activity of the Inquisition continued intermittently until the sixteenth century. The function of its modern representative, the Congregation of the Holy Office, is to inquire into the orthodoxy of books, and to condemn them, if they be found to contain any doctrine contrary to faith or morals.—Our adversaries point to the Ecclesiastical Inquisition as a proof of the intolerance and cruelty of the Church. (1) As to the charge of intolerance:—A man is said to tolerate what he believes to be an error when he, though able, is unwilling to suppress it. The Church, commissioned by Christ to preach the Gospel, and clothed with infallibility, can never be unwilling to suppress erroneous doctrine. The Church and every lover of truth must necessarily be intolerant of error. The so-called tolerance of the present age is not tolerance in the strict sense. It is due either to the incapacity to persecute, or to utter indifferentism in religious matters. (2) As to the charge of cruelty:—(a) "The Church, established by Christ as a perfect society, is empowered to make laws and inflict penalties for their violation. Heresy not only violates her law but strikes at her very life, unity of belief."[23] (b) "When Christianity became the religion of the Empire, and still more when the peoples of Northern Europe became Christian nations, the close alliance of Church and State made unity of faith essential not only to the ecclesiastical organization, but also to civil society. Heresy, in consequence, was a crime which secular rulers were bound in duty to punish. It was regarded as worse than any other crime, even that of high treason; it was for society in those times what we call anarchy."[23] Still, it is an undoubted fact that for centuries "the principal teachers of the Church.... shrank from such stern measures against heresy as torture and capital punishment,"[23] and yielded only under pressure from the civil powers. Hence, it cannot be said that the Inquisition was due solely to the initiative of the Church. (c) The Inquisition gave the heretic ample time to recant. Its officers were bound

---

[23] See Cath. Encycl. "The Inquisition."

under most severe penalties to move by slow delays so as to give the accused every opportunity of escape. Whereas the civil authority, when it acted, as it often did, without any reference to the Church, gave no time for repentance. The Inquisition, therefore, was milder in its methods than the secular courts. (*d*) Protestants, in the days of the Inquisition, dealt with their opponents exactly as Catholics dealt with theirs. But, while the severity of Protestants was indefensible, since they maintained the liberty of private judgment and, therefore, admitted that their victim might be right and they themselves wrong, the severity of Catholics, on the other hand, was consistent with their doctrine that they alone possess Divine truth, and that the heretic is necessarily a source of moral or spiritual infection, a slayer of souls, and, therefore, more dangerous than the thief or the murderer. (*e*) The criminal law of the Middle Ages was much more severe than that of the present day, the death penalty being exacted for burglary, blasphemy, and even petty theft. From the modern standpoint, those in truth were merciless times. But what of the boasted clemency of our own enlightened age? A future generation may pass a most severe judgment on us for our indifference to the inhuman conditions in which so many of our workers toil and live, and for our cruelty in casting appalling multitudes of our children into the raging furnace of war. (*f*) Let us suppose all the facts alleged under the charge of cruelty to be fully established. Let us accept as true all the gross exaggerations of unprincipled adversaries as to the number of the victims of the Inquisition, and the nature of the punishments to which they were subjected. What follows? Nothing against the Church as a Divine institution.[24] Nothing against her claim to doctrinal Infallibility. Much, perhaps, against the personal wisdom and clemency of her rulers. But, even though such personal failure be admitted—and in view of all the circumstances of the times we are far from admitting it—it serves but to emphasize the fact that the weakness and errors of individuals can never bring the Church to ruin.

*The Spanish Inquisition.*—When Protestants speak of the cruelty of the Catholic Church, they usually have in mind the proceedings of the Spanish Inquisition, a tribunal established by Ferdinand and Isabella in 1481, at the request of their subjects and with the approval of the Holy See. Its purpose was to unmask and punish pretended converts from Judaism or Mohammedanism. Many of these possessed great wealth and influence, and held high office in the State and even in the Church. Their plots and secret machi-

---

[24] Consider the dread punishments inflicted by God under the Old Law (see, *e.g.*, 1 Kings vi. 19; 2 K. vi. 7), and the deaths of Ananias and Saphira under the New (see Acts v.)

nations threatened to reverse the dearly bought victory which the Spaniards had won over the Moors after a struggle of nearly eight centuries. The Inquisitors were ecclesiastics, but they held office at the pleasure of the Spanish crown. Pope Sixtus IV., who declared that his sanction for the erection of the tribunal had been obtained on false pretences, protested more than once, but without avail, against its severity. Since it was a political rather than an ecclesiastical institution, the Church cannot be held responsible for its proceedings.[25]

**Outside the Church there is no Salvation.**—God commands all men to be members of His Church.[26] Those who deliberately disobey Him will be lost eternally. But, since He condemns no man except for a grave fault, He will not condemn those who through inculpable ignorance are unaware of His precept, who serve Him faithfully according to their conscience, who have a sincere desire to do His will, and, therefore, implicitly, the desire to become members of His Church. Let us consider the following cases:— (1) A man, born of Protestant parents, is baptized; lives all his life a Protestant, without ever having a grave doubt that he is in the wrong; makes, before death, an act of perfect contrition for grave sins committed or an act of perfect charity.—Such a man will be saved, for he dies in the state of grace. (2) A heathen has never heard even the name of Christ; he obeys the natural law according to his lights; he dies a heathen, to all appearances.— The Divine Mercy will not suffer such a man to be lost. It is a recognized principle that God, because He wills that all be saved, does not deny grace to him who does his best. He will infallibly give him who is faithful to the natural law sufficient illumination and aid to enable him to make the acts of faith and charity necessary for salvation. The act of charity includes the desire of full compliance with the Divine Will; it includes, therefore, the desire of baptism.—In view of the fact that the Church stands plainly before the eyes of men like a city on a mountain-top, that the words of her ministers have gone forth to the ends of the earth, we do not venture to say that such cases as these are typical of large numbers. We are certain, at all events, that for men, deprived of the abundant graces at the disposal of those who belong

---

[25] Llorente, the chief witness on whom Protestants rely, was appointed Secretary to the Inquisition at Madrid, in 1789, but lost his position some years later through his misconduct. His work, *A Critical History of the Inquisition*, was prompted by a desire of revenge. Apart from his undoubted animus, the fact that he destroyed the records on which he purported to base his statistics involves his testimony in grave suspicion.

[26] See Ch. IX.

to the visible membership of the Church, salvation is not easy. (3) Children who die unbaptized are, according to the common teaching, admitted to a state of natural, but not supernatural, happiness. The Church has never said that they are sent to eternal punishment.

**Church and State.**—The Church provides for the spiritual, the State for the temporal interests of man. Each derives its authority, or right to command, from God. Each is independent and supreme in its own sphere; each is provided with all the powers necessary for the attainment of its end; each is, therefore, what is termed a perfect society. Matters purely spiritual, *e.g.*, Divine worship, the education of the clergy, belong exclusively to the Church; matters purely temporal, *e.g.*, the choice of a form of government, the development of industries, exclusively to the State. Matters of a mixed character which affect both societies alike should be dealt with by mutual arrangement, but in case of conflict, the State, in as much as it pursues the less important end, must yield to the Church. Though directly concerned with spirituals alone, the Church is obviously entitled to all temporal aids necessary, or useful, for the success of her mission: she is entitled, *e.g.*, to build churches and seminaries, to collect revenue, and to conduct schools for the education of the laity.[27]

Since there can be no lasting temporal prosperity without sound morality, and since there can be no sound morality without true religion, the Church maintains that it is not only the duty, but the

---

[27] Christ gave the Church authority to teach; hence, also, authority to protect her children from false teaching: " Feed my lambs," etc. The deepest impressions on mind and character are made in early life. The morals and religious convictions of a teacher, apart from any positive instruction he may give on religion, the general surroundings and atmosphere of the school, and the precise course of secular knowledge pursued there, exercise a very great influence for good or evil on the whole future of a child in his relation to God and the Church. The command to " feed my lambs " has, therefore, given the Church authority in educational matters, authority to conduct schools herself, authority to safeguard the interests of her children in schools conducted by others, authority to supervise the selection of teachers and text-books, and to condemn any school or educational system hostile to the faith. Pope Pius IX. has declared the following proposition contrary to Catholic doctrine : " The whole government of the Public Schools in which Christian youth are educated can and ought to be in the hands of the civil authority, and so completely in their hands that no right of any other authority is recognized to interfere with school discipline, with the order of studies, with the conferring of degrees, with the selection of the teacher." (Prop. 45.)

interest of the State, (1) to respect the law of God and the Church in all its enactments; (2) to be subject to the Church in all spiritual matters; (3) to discharge, through the ministers of the Church, its debt of public worship;[28] (4) to protect the Church, to promote her interests, and, in general, (5) to act in perfect harmony with her. Such is the ideal for which the Church strives; in countries predominantly Catholic, she urges her claim for its realization; elsewhere, she refrains from doing so, and is, as a rule, content, from motives of prudence, to demand nothing more than liberty of worship, and such protection as is usually accorded to private societies within the State. She has expressly declared that the separation of Church from State is an evil, and that she admits it only with a view to avoid greater evil.

*Definition.*—*The Church is the congregation of all the faithful who, being baptised, profess the same faith, partake of the same sacraments and sacrifice, and are governed by their lawful pastors, under one supreme head, the Pope, the Vicar of Christ.*

[Read : *The See of St. Peter*, Allies, C.T.S., price 1s. 10d.; *Authority*, Rev. Luke Rivington, C.T.S., price 1s. 2d.; *The First Eight General Councils and Papal Infallibility*, Dom Chapman, O.S.B., C.T.S., price 7d.; *Talks about St. Peter*, Fr. Bampfield, C.T.S. (four pamphlets), 1d. each; *Galileo*, Fr. Hull, S.J., C.T.S., price 7d.]

---

[28] See Ch. III.

# APPENDIX.

## CHRIST, A LIVING FORCE: AN ARGUMENT FOR HIS DIVINITY.

Newman represents Napoleon in the solitude of his imprisonment as communing with himself, thus[29]:—

"I have been accustomed to put before me the examples of Alexander and Cæsar, with the hope of rivalling their exploits, and living in the minds of men for ever. Yet, after all, in what sense does Cæsar, in what sense does Alexander live? At best, nothing but their names is known. ... Nay, even their names do but flit up and down the world like ghosts, mentioned only on particular occasions, or from accidental associations. Their chief home is the schoolroom; they have a foremost place in boys' grammars and exercise books. ... So low is heroic Alexander fallen, so low is imperial Cæsar, 'ut pueris placeat et declamatio fiat.'

"But, on the contrary, there is just one Name in the whole world that lives; it is the Name of One who passed His years in obscurity, and who died a malefactor's death. Eighteen hundred years have gone since that time, but still it has its hold on the human mind. It has possessed the world, and it maintains possession. Amid the most varied nations, under the most diversified circumstances, in the most cultivated, in the rudest races and intellects, in all classes of society, the Owner of that great Name reigns. High and low, rich and poor, acknowledge Him. Millions of souls are conversing with Him, are venturing on His word, are looking for His Presence. Palaces, sumptuous, innumerable are raised to His honour; His image, as in the hour of His deepest humiliation, is triumphantly displayed in the proud city, in the open country, in the corners of streets, on the tops of mountains. It sanctifies the ancestral hall, and the bedchamber; it is the subject for the exercise of the highest genius in the imitative arts. It is worn next the heart in life; it is held before the failing eyes in death. Here, then, is One who is *not* a mere name, who is not a mere fiction, who is a reality. He is dead and gone, but still He lives,—lives as a living, energetic thought of successive generations, as the awful motive power of a thousand great events. He has done without effort what others with life-long struggles have not done. Can He be less than Divine? Who is He but the Creator Himself, who is sovereign over His own works, towards whom our eyes and hearts turn instinctively, because He is our Father and our God?"

---

[29] *Grammar of Assent*, p. 490-1.—The argument was Napoleon's, the words are Newman's.

## SUPPLEMENTARY NOTES

**The Proofs for the existence of God.**—(1) In re-reading these proofs with more advanced pupils, the teacher should emphasise Argument IV. and link up with it the paragraph on Infinity, p. 19.

(2) The following proof of the Infinity of God may be added: We get the measure of a sculptor's ability by comparing the finished statue with the rude block of marble. His ability is in proportion to the distance he places between the perfect work of art and the unshapen stone. The greater the distance, the greater the ability. Now, the Divine Artificer had no material on which to begin His work. The things He made were nothing until He made them. But the distance between "nothing" and actual existence is infinite. God, therefore, in creating, has produced something which is at an infinite distance from its previous state. Such an act is infinite, and can come only from an Infinite Being.

(3) Attention is directed to footnote [71], p. 69, where it is shown that the Resurrection of Christ enables us to dispense with all philosophical proof for the existence of God.

**The Spirituality of the Soul.** OBJECTION: "The mind cannot act, if the brain be injured. Therefore, it follows that brain and mind are one and the same, and that what we describe as acts of the mind are merely movements of the brain."

REPLY: (1) The conclusion cannot be sound. The brain is matter. Abstract ideas, reasoning, and free-will, are immaterial things. They have no extension. They are utterly distinct from matter, and cannot be identified with it or with any of its states, whether rest or motion.

(2) The conclusion does not follow. In the living man, soul and body are most intimately united together. Every act of the one is accompanied by some act or movement of the other. The soul cannot think without some accompanying movement of the brain. Hence, in the ordinary course of nature, thought becomes impossible, if the brain be seriously injured, or if, as in sleep and unconsciousness, its proper activity be impeded. But does this make thought identical with a movement of the brain? By no means, as the following illustration will show: Suppose a lighted candle to be set in a lantern with a rather dim pane of glass. The candle, though burning with uniform brightness, will show only as much of its light as the glass allows to pass through. If the glass be thoroughly blackened, no light will be seen. As long, therefore, as the candle remains in the lantern, its lighting-power will depend on, but obviously will not be identical with, the transparency of the glass. Now, the soul may be compared to the lighted candle, the body to the lantern, and the brain to the glass. While the soul is in the body, it cannot think unless the brain be in a suitable condition. Further, as the candle, when removed from the lantern with its imperfectly transparent pane of glass, will shed all the better light, so, too, the soul, when released from the body at death, will be able to exhibit a higher activity of thought.[1]

---

[1] *Cf.* Bishop Vaughan, *Life after Death*, London, Washbourne, 2s. 3d.

# INDEX TO PART 1.

Acts of the Apostles, 47.
Agnosticism, doctrine of, 20, 23 ; advocates of, 23.
Alison, quoted, 114.
Ammianus Marcellinus, 71.
Animals, lower, how they differ from men, 27-29 ; instinct of, 5, 28 n. 4.
Apostles, mission of, 75.
Aristotle, 33.
Atheism, forms of : Materialism, Pantheism, Agnosticism, 22-24.

Baur, 47.
Belief, universal : argument from, 10-15.
Bible, not the sole rule of faith, 99, 100.
Branch Theory, The, 102-3.
Buddhism, 115.

Calvin, 98.
Celsus, 42, 69.
Chalcedon, Council of, 122.
Charles V., Emperor of Germany 96 n. 2.
Christ—His Divinity proved : I. By His perfection as a man (54-59) and as a teacher of natural religion (60-63), viewed in the light of His claim to be God (49-53). II. By His Resurrection (64-69). III. By His miracles (70), by His prophecies (70-71), by the fact that He was Himself the fulfilment of prophecy (71-72). Other proofs : I. From the rapid propagation of Christianity (89-91), and the constancy of the Martyrs (91-93). II. From the unity of the Church (109). III. From the fact that He is still a living force, 137.—See, also, Note at top of p. 40—The Mission of Christ, 74.—See *Church*.
Church : a society founded by Christ, 77-8 ; its characteristics — imperishable, apostolic, one, universal, visible holy, and infallible, 79-88.—Method of identifying the true Church, 94. Catholic Church alone has all the marks of the true Church : (1) it claims infallibility ; (2) it claims apostolicity ; (3) it is universal or catholic and at the same time one— one in government, faith and worship ; (4) it is holy. Stability of Catholic Church, 110f.—Church and State, 135f.
Cicero, 12.
Classics, genuineness of, 45 n. 14.
Constantine Emperor, 89.
Contingence, argument from, 17.
Causes, physical : inadequacy of, as final explanation, 14.

Energy, conservation of, 37 ; dissipation of, 9.
Ephesus, Council of, 121.

Fabre, 28 n. 4.
Faith, Deposit of, 88 ; Protestant and Catholic rules of, 99, 100.
Free will, 27.

Galileo, 129f.
Gladstone, 114
God, existence of : proved (1) from the Laws of Nature ; (2) from the Universal Belief of Mankind ; (3) from the

## INDEX TO PART I.

Origin of Mind; (4) from Contingence, 1-19.—Nature of: Simplicity, Spirituality, Infinity, Unity, Omnipotence, Omnipresence, Omniscience, Incomprehensibility, 19-21.—See *Christ*.

Gospels, genuineness proved by external and internal evidence, 41-45; integrity, chiefly by the reverence of the early Christians for the sacred text, 45; veracity, by the character and history of the Evangelists, and the impossibility of fraud, 46.— Synoptic, 41 n. 1; Harnack's opinion of, 48.—See *Christ*.

Greek Church, The Schismatic: its divisions and origin, 100; its doctrines, 101; not the true Church, 101-2.

Greek, Hellenistic, 44.

Haeckel, 7, 8, 22.
Harnack, 48, 63.
Heredity as explanation of instinct, 28 n. 4.
Honorius, Pope, 131.
Hume, 36.
Huxley, 23, 129 n. 18.
Hypnotism, 38, 70.

Infallibility, subject and object of, 88; objections against, 109-10.
Inquisition, Ecclesiastical, 131-3; Spanish, 133f.

Jerusalem, attempt to rebuild temple of, 71.
Josephus, 44 n. 10, 71, 72.
Judaism, Divine origin of, 73.
Julian the Apostate, 71.

Kant, 62.
Kelvin, Lord, 9.
Knowledge of material and abstract things, 25, 26.

Lecky, 59.
Liberius, Pope, 130f.
Luther, 97, 98, 130.

Macaulay, quoted, 111, 112.
Manning, Cardinal, 103 n. 13.
Martyrs, constancy of, 91-3.
Materialism, its advocates, 22: its doctrine, 6. See *Causes*.
Matter, animate and inanimate, 2-4; basic, 18.
Melanchthon, 130.
Mind, argument from origin of 15.—See *Soul*.
Miracles, signs of revelation, 35; objections against (1) from insufficiency of evidence, (2) opposition to physical science (3) possibility of non-Divine authorship, 36-38;—a sign of the sanctity of the Church, 86; found in the Catholic Church, 108.
Missions, Protestant and Catholic, 105 n. 16.
Mivart, St. G., quoted, 9.
Mohammedanism, 116.
Müller, Max, 12.
Muratori, Fragment of, 47.

Nature, law of, 2 n.1; argument from laws of, 1-10.
Newman, 91, 114, 137.
Newton, 2, 6, 21.

Pantheism, its advocates and doctrine, 23.
Papacy, stability of, 110.
Papias, 42.
Peschel, 12.
Pharisees, 56, 57, 61, 72.
Plato, 33.
Pliny, 89.
Plutarch, 12.
Pope, Primacy of, 118-123; Infallibility of, 124-127; twofold teaching authority of, 128; objections against Infallibility, 128-131.
Protestantism: its divisions, 95; its origin, 95-7; its

doctrines, 97-8; not the true Church, 98-100.

Rationalism, 36 obj. 2.
Reformation, causes of, 96, 97; doctrines of, 97, 98.
Religion, Christian, excellence of, 39; revelation of, attested by many miracles and prophecies, 38.—Natural, individual and social duties of, to God, 31-32; duties of, to oneself, to one's neighbour, 32; knowledge of, practically unattainable, and useless, if attained, 33, 34; insufficiency of, an argument for probability of, Revelation, 34.
Resurrection, 64-66. Objections: Deception, Trance, and Hallucination Hypotheses, 66-68.—Objection of Celsus, 69.

Salvation, doctrine of exclusive, 134.
Scientists, believers in a Personal God, 22.
Socrates, 62.
Soul, Spirituality of, 25-30; Immortality of, 31.
Stoics, 33, 90.
Strauss, 47, 68.
St. Augustine, 45, n. 13; 67.
„ Basil, 122.
„ Clement (Pope), 41, 80, 123.
„ Cyril of Alexandria, 122.
„ Irenaeus, 42, 80.
„ Jerome, 45 n. 13, 122.
„ Justin, 42, 89.
„ Paul, epistles of, opinions of adversaries concerning, 47.

Tacitus, 65 n. 56; 89.
Tatian, 42.
Tertullian, 42.
Tyndall, 7.

www.ingramcontent.com/pod-product-compliance
Lightning Source LLC
Chambersburg PA
CBHW010918040426
42444CB00016B/3438